*SIMULATIONS IN
ENGLISH TEACHING*

Open University Press

English, Language, and Education series

SELECTED TITLES IN THE SERIES

The Problem with Poetry
Richard Andrews

Writing Development
Roslyn Arnold

Simulations in English Teaching
Paul Bambrough

Writing Policy in Action
Eve Bearne and Cath Farrow

Secondary Worlds
Michael Benton

Thinking Through English
Paddy Creber

Teaching Secondary English
David Curtis

Developing English
Peter Dougill (ed.)

The Primary Language Book (2nd Edition)
Peter Dougill

Reading Against Racism
Emrys Evans (ed.)

English Teaching and Media Education
Andrew Goodwyn

English at the Core
Peter Griffith

Literary Theory and English Teaching
Peter Griffith

Lesbian and Gay Issues in the English Classroom
Simon Harris

Reading and Response
Mike Hayhoe and Stephen Parker (eds)

General Editor: Anthony Adams
Lecturer in Education, University of Cambridge

Reassessing Language and Literacy
Mike Hayhoe and Stephen Parker (eds)

Who Owns English?
Mike Hayhoe and Stephen Parker (eds)

Language and the English Curriculum
John Keen

Shakespeare in the Classroom
Susan Leach

Developing Readers in the Middle Years
Elaine Millard

Language Awareness for Teachers
Bill Mittins

The Making of English Teachers
Robert Protherough and Judith Atkinson

Young People Reading
Charles Sarland

School Writing
Yanina Sheeran and Douglas Barnes

Playing the Language Game
Valerie Shepherd

Reading Narrative as Literature
Andrew Stibbs

Reading Within and Beyond the Classroom
Dan Taverner

Reading for Real
Barrie Wade (ed.)

Spoken English Illuminated
Andrew Wilkinson, Alan Davies and Deborah Berrill

SIMULATIONS IN ENGLISH TEACHING

Paul Bambrough

Open University Press
Buckingham · Philadelphia

Open University Press
Celtic Court
22 Ballmoor
Buckingham
MK18 1XW

and
1900 Frost Road, Suite 101
Bristol, PA 19007, USA

First Published 1994

Copyright © Paul J. Bambrough 1994

All rights reserved. Except for the quotation of short passages for the purposes of criticism and review, no part of this publication may be reproduced, stored in a retrieval system, or transmitted, in any form or by any means, electronic, mechanical, photocopying, recording or otherwise, without the prior written permission of the publisher or a licence from the Copyright Licensing Agency Limited. Details of such licences (for reprographic reproduction) may be obtained from the Copyright Licensing Agency Ltd of 90 Tottenham Court Road, London, W1P 9HE.

A catalogue record of this book is available from the British Library

ISBN 0 335 19151 7

Library of Congress Cataloging-in-Publication Data
Bambrough, Paul J. (Paul John), 1958–
    Simulations in English teaching / Paul J. Bambrough.
      p.   cm. — (English, language, and education series)
    Includes bibliographical references and index.
    ISBN 0–335–19151–7 (pb)
    1. English language—Study and teaching—Simulation methods.
I. Title. II. Series.
LB1576.B27 1994
418'.007—dc20   94–12227
                                                                     CIP

Typeset by Type Study, Scarborough
Printed in Great Britain by St Edmundsbury Press Ltd,
Bury St Edmunds, Suffolk

For Kay and Imogen

Contents

General editor's introduction   9
Acknowledgements   12

1. **An introduction to simulations**   13
2. **Designing simulations for English teaching**   20
    Part A: First Steps   21
    Part B: Nuts and bolts and building regulations   28
3. **Designing a simulation:** *Roll of Thunder*   40
4. **Running the simulation**   68
5. **The debrief**   75
6. **The language experience**   84
7. **Issues of control and reality**   98

References   102
Index   104

General editor's introduction

Many English teachers have been using various forms of games and simulations in their teaching for some time. This has often taken the form of a 'one off' event with no clear rationale behind it. Although there have been a number of books dealing with the use of simulations in communications courses and they are well established as a technique in both management training and EFL teaching, there has been no recent book in this country that deals with the use of simulations as a natural form for the organization of English work. The present text sets out to meet this need. There is a clear need for more books that look at simulations, not in general terms but in relation to specific curriculum areas. While this volume takes English teaching at its centre, its discussion is largely applicable to other areas of the humanities curriculum also.

My own experience of the use of simulations in the classroom, at both secondary and tertiary level, has been that the form provides a convenient way in which to bring together a number of different language skills within a significant event. Provided the initial briefing is adequately conducted a high level of motivation usually results; moreover, in a well planned simulation, the teacher is usually able to observe rather than take a central part as the simulation gets underway. Such observation is, of course, essential to provide material for the debrief that follows the simulation. However, in the present National Curriculum climate in England and Wales, with its demands for assessment, simulations have the added advantage that they provide an opportunity for the teacher to stand back from the classroom and observe student work for assessment purposes. In many simulations this is especially true in the difficult area of the assessment of speaking and listening. Simulations should therefore have a particularly valuable part to play in today's classrooms.

I stress the need for the simulation to fit into normal elements of the English curriculum rather than be a 'one off' event. Students who take part in simulations tend to see the technique as something unique in itself. Having 'done' one simulation, they do not always see the point of doing another.

Simulations are one of a number of classroom techniques to be used as, and when, appropriate to the curriculum content.

The experience of students in most simulations concentrates most upon the affective and psycho-motor processes, but, finally, in much teaching it is the cognitive gains and understandings that are important also. Hence the vital significance of the 'debrief' which should help the students to come to terms with what they have *learned* as a result of the simulation. The teacher's evaluation of every simulation, on which will be based the decision whether to use it again, in its present or modified form, must take account of this learning process and the effectiveness of the simulation in achieving it. To imagine that the simulation has been successful simply because the class has 'enjoyed it' is to devalue the technique itself.

However, cognitive gain is not everything. Part of what we have to engage with as English teachers is certainly the area of social learning. Students, at all levels from infant school to tertiary education, need to learn to work cooperatively in groups, to engage with and support each other. The simulation is a powerful tool for learning these skills and I would certainly see the intermixture of affective and socio-dynamic learning which it involves as an important part of any simulation. Students will need to get angry at times, to feel under pressure, to divest themselves of powerful feelings; but always with the safeguard that these experiences are undergone 'in role', in the simulated as opposed to the 'real' world. However, when they come out of role, it may be that the 'reality' is informed and changed by the experience of the simulation. Hence, for example, the popularity of using simulation techniques with much educational material which has been prepared to help students understand the problems of the third world.

Possibly because it is so powerful a vehicle, the literature concerning simulations (which, in general terms, is very wide-ranging) is marked by disagreements amongst theorists in the field. These extend even to seemingly simple issues of definition: what, for example, is the difference between a 'simulation' and a 'game'? The two terms are often, in my view mistakenly, used as if they were synonymous but, if they are different, in what ways do they differ and what different educational purposes do they serve? What also are the relationships between simulations and drama; to what extent does the role play, with which both are concerned, take on different forms and serve different purposes?

There is also the highly controversial set of issues around the role of the teacher in the context of a simulation. How is it changed from a conventional role? Is the teacher as 'controller' different from the teacher *qua* teacher? What of such issues as authority and control, and, especially, the ownership of the classroom events?

If the simulation is going to grow out of the curriculum needs of the teaching and the everyday work of the classroom, it is unlikely that any of the commercially produced simulations which are available will exactly fit the teacher's needs. Thus the necessity to find ways of devising one's own simulations with a sufficient understanding of the form to know that they have a reasonable chance of working the first time they are used. There have been books before on how to create simulations but the present volume is the first of which I am aware that tackles this task head on in terms of the needs of the English teacher. In its careful discussion of the various stages involved in the creation of an original simulation, the 'nuts and bolts' of the business so to speak, the present volume makes a useful, original, and practical addition to the busy teacher's bookshelf. Alongside the scholarship that informs its pages there is a sense of classroom reality that makes it a really useful 'handbook', a do-it-yourself guide to the art of simulation. It may be best read by whole Departments as part of an in-service exercise.

In commending this book to its readership, I hope that readers will not only be informed by its contents but also inspired and confident enough to put its principles into practice.

Anthony Adams

Acknowledgements

My thanks to Springfield County Middle School, Milton Keynes, and to Samuel Whitbread, Shefford, for letting me on the premises!

1 An introduction to simulations

What is a simulation?

Imagine you are walking along a school corridor. The door to the first classroom you come to is open. Amidst a chaos of riotous noise you can discern the occasional comment:

> No way! That's not fair! You haven't even listened to our arguments!
> But my proposals are unquestionable. I am simply acting in your interests. This project will be good for you.
> Rubbish. You're simply out for yourself! This won't be of any benefit to us.

You peer discreetly peer around the edge of the door as a chorus of cheers goes up in support, presumably, of the last statement. About twenty children, sitting in rows of chairs without a table in sight, are vociferously engaging a lone figure facing them at the front of the classroom. The children look angry, frustrated – the figure at the front close to despair. On the wall behind him is a notice board with a banner across its top 'Town Hall Notices'. Several scraps of paper pinned to the board announce forthcoming events, including one rather bolder than the rest declaring:

Public enquiry into the proposed siting of a sewage works at Yardley End

Chaired by Sir Norman Findle

To be held at Heversham Town Hall

11.00 a.m. June 8 1994

In simulations, participants have roles. In this simulation, the roles were those of villagers and a representative from the water board. What makes a simulation different from other role activities is that the roles function within a *structure* which represents a real or actual situation, and that the elements of this situation are represented consistently in a *dynamic* or ongoing way. For this activity to be termed a simulation, it would not have been enough for the teacher to have said:

> Right. You, you and you are people who live in this village called Heversham. You're a representative of the Water Board. OK. You (pointing to the representative of the Water Board) want to build a sewage works next to the village. Fight it out. This notice board will keep your mind on things.

The function of the roles cannot be defined by sudden inspirational guesswork on the part of participants in a vacuum of information. It must be defined by the ongoing structure based on the actual situation or system represented. The roles would have been based on roles in that situation or system and their behaviour would have been determined according to the behaviour one would expect in the real or actual situation. So if we take the example above, the *structure* is based on a public inquiry into the building of a sewage works near a village. The behaviour of the roles would be defined by this issue and by the rules and procedures of such an inquiry and not in the broader sense of, for example, how the publican in the village feels about the new shopkeeper (unless this has bearing on the building of the sewage works).

The designer of the simulation would have included information about the role and its function, the nature of the problem, opportunities and structures for communication, relationships of power and function between this role and others in the simulation, and evidence or information critical to the issue here as this information might be available in the actual situation. One would not expect a villager to suddenly invent evidence that a plague which would wipe out the entire world had been identified to arise from this type of sewage works. Common knowledge might have been provided as evidence about the project in the form of newspaper reports and some roles might have had information that others didn't, but this would have been determined by the simulation designer, *not* by the participant.

Having been provided with the structure, the participant then functions *autonomously* without the help of the teacher or controller (who runs the simulation). The objective may be to see how the participant copes with the system in which she operates, or to develop skills to cope with this system, or to learn about the system itself. The latter may include trying to understand how people normally feel who have to exist in such a situation (empathy). The objectives will depend on the structure of the simulation and we will return to this.

The introduction of these situations in the form of simulations into the classroom represents both an attempt to bring the real world to the classroom and, linked to this, to introduce a process- rather than instruction-based methodology. It is in this sense that autonomy, enabled by the structure of the simulation, is critical. Students experience decision-making situations for themselves – as town planners or business operators – and learn from their *own* successes and failures. A debrief usually follows a simulation and it is during this that problems and approaches can be deconstructed and learning can be consolidated.

The simulation differs from some other forms of role play in that one is not asking the participants to take on the roles or attributes of characters other than themselves. This might be the case with some role activities; for example, in the exploration of a text or in some psychodrama, one might use role to ask, 'How would Othello behave when arrested for shoplifting?' Nor would feelings be directly attributed: 'Come on let's see some anger!' One is not working from a script (drama in the performance sense), for there is no plot to a simulation except that which emerges from the interaction of the participants in each run. Such approaches, which have value in their own right, would simply take the use of role closer to instruction and prescription. None of the participants in the simulation above would have been told to feel angry or to take a point of view or to make particular decisions. They would have arrived at the moment we visited only as a result of how they perceived their role in relation to the problem and the ongoing circumstances in which they found themselves; they may have been incensed by newspaper reports or they may have exerted themselves because of powers they *found* themselves to have.

A key advantage to using simulations in the classroom is that they are highly motivating. Good simulations engage students intensely. This is largely because their motivation is intrinsic. It is not that of the teacher requiring work or offering some extrinsic reward. The reward is entirely intrinsic. The participant comes to believe in her role and the task, and the accomplishment of the task becomes her primary function. This motivation is not simply the motivation of role play, but is a product of the reality which is constructed from the structured environment, of the power to control this environment, and of the dynamic of the simulation which draws the participant in more and more. In addition, removing the teacher from the instructor–instructee frame removes a fear from students of doing things wrong, allowing them to take risks and function freely. Chapter 6 examines the case of two students who found the motivation of the world of the simulation irresistible.

Systems simulations and communications simulations

For the purposes of this book, I want to make a distinction between two kinds of simulation (these are by no means the only distinctions possible), although these might be seen as two ends of a continuum. The distinction will serve the reader in helping to understand the purposes, implications and design of simulations, which are discussed in later chapters.

The simulation about the sewage works which I have described had a communicative reality. That is, the interaction taking place would have been the interaction of the public inquiry with all the social and behavioural rules and conventions of that particular system. Participants would have explored a whole range of responses to the issue through 'real' interactive situations, perhaps the organization of a television debate or a demonstration. In functional terms, you get the actual behaviour of the villagers and the actual situation being simulated. Only the physical environment of the classroom (or surprising youth of the participants) might distinguish this from the real situation. These are often referred to as *role play* simulations. For good reasons, Jones (1987: 13) has challenged the 'play' part of this term as suggesting 'mimicry' or pretence rather than intrinsic motivation. I shall refer to these kinds of simulation as 'communications' simulations, since they are designed to achieve communicative reality, although communication naturally takes place in most simulations involving human participants. The objective of this kind of simulation is likely to be the development of communication skills (or the assessment of these), though this need not be exclusively the case.

At the other end of the continuum are what I shall term 'systems' simulations. These are simulations like *Monopoly* or *Blood Money* (which I refer to below). The communicative/social/interactive reality is of secondary significance to the system being represented. In *Monopoly*, for example, an economic system is represented, but because of the compression of this system, *Monopoly* cannot explore the actual boardroom meetings or allow for real-life transactions to take place every time a property is exchanged (as might have occurred in the simulation based on the sewage works proposal). To do so would mean the process taking years.

Of a similar nature in this respect is Greenblat's simulation called *Blood Money*, which explores the problems faced by haemophiliacs in obtaining adequate medical care and in trying to lead 'normal' lives. The social and economic problems include loss of work due to illness and unavailability of medical provision at the right time. There is seen to be a set of causal relationships between elements in the system – for example, illness leads to poor work record leads to unemployment leads to poorer health – and these are translated into a more compressed form. Work is represented in the throwing of darts at a dartboard, for example. Poor health affecting work takes the form of throwing darts while seated. Lack of medical provision means waiting in queues until you are given a clean bill of health so that you can throw your darts standing up.

Both simulations use tokens for behaviour and interaction – the throwing of darts or the movement of pieces around a board in place of the actual behaviour or interaction. The decisions taken by participants may be from a role perspective (business operator) and be of the kind one would normally make within the system represented (buying and selling houses), but the interaction is tokenistic. These are still both simulations, but they are not primarily communications simulations. Sometimes a simulation may combine a systems approach with communicative reality, although there may be problems in doing so – these are considered in Chapter 3, where I look at the design process for a systems simulation.

The author exercises a considerable amount of control over the structure with these systems simulations. The game of *Monopoly* and Greenblat's *Blood Money* contain 'a large number of variables' (Thatcher and Robinson 1986: 26) which predefine options for behaviour and the range of possible outcomes according to the system represented, thus limiting participant control over these. The variables are usually translated from a detailed model of the real-world system which would go something like:

> if a and b then c   *or*   if a then b then c or d

If a haemophiliac can't get medical help, then they work less efficiently and then they may not be employed. This kind of simulation creates understanding of, and empathy with, the system by being pushed largely 'from pillar to post' by the system dynamic. A possible range of real-life consequences of actions, as they are seen to exist by the simulation author, are built in.

The communications simulation based on the sewage works would have exercised much less author control, beyond, put simply, the provision of roles, a problem, and information relating to these for participants to act on. Participants would have had much more freedom to make decisions according to the interaction that had taken place and *their* interpretation of the social norms and powers that might be attributed to the situation.

There are important implications and issues arising from this distinction. Apart from the different learning objectives (or emphases on these) which I have touched on here and which are discussed further in the chapters that follow, the different forms of simulation impact on both design, which is discussed in Chapter 2, and on issues of control, which are discussed in the final chapter.

Reality and the role of simulations in English teaching

Simulations have become identified with real-world experience, because they have enabled the real world to be studied (or participants in that world to be studied) where this could not be done in reality. A pilot can be trained in the flight simulator without personal risk or expense in loss of aircraft. I can also enjoy the same experience on the computer I am now working at, together with car racing simulations, at a fraction of the cost of the real experience. Real-world systems can also be studied by being compressed into simulations allowing the experience which could not otherwise take place. Coleman describes the use of simulations in terms of studying social systems through this kind of compression (in Taylor and Walford 1978: 20):

> The game may provide for him [the student] that degree of abstraction from life and simplification of life that allows him to understand better certain fundamentals of social education . . .

Indeed, this is precisely what Greenblat's *Blood Money* does, as I have shown. This might be the only way a doctor or government minister could come to appreciate fully the logistical difficulties of, and the emotional trauma of, those affected by this real-world system.

It is not just simplification and abstraction, or saving risk and expense in the form of systems simulations, which have tied the identity of simulations to the real world. Communications simulations, too, have been used to examine real-world environments, for example through the use of role interaction to develop management skills.

Definitions of simulations thus abound with this connection with reality, including:

> A simulation is a scaled-down, simplified model of reality; it imitates a dynamic process that occurs in the real world.
> (Davis and Hollowell 1977: v)

> [The simulation is] . . . an operational representation of the central features of reality.
> (Guetzkow, in Thatcher and Robinson 1986: 15)

> Participants take on roles which are representations of roles in the *real* world.
> (Taylor and Walford 1978: 7)

Simulations in education seem inextricably linked to the real world as a means to overcome the 'irrelevance' of learning in schools to life beyond school. This kind of thinking was defined in particular in the early days of simulations when this concern was more justified. Taylor and Walford (1978: 36–7), for example, described how 'schoolwork seems divorced from the real world' and simulations give the student 'a chance to sample the real world'. Sharrock and Watson (1987: 36) also describe how simulations 'were seen as one of several ways . . . of bringing the classroom into close contact and correspondence with the practical realities of "the world outside"'.

Jones (1987: 10) has argued that 'plausibility and consistency' are more important than 'attempts to reproduce the real world'. His concern is more with 'reality of function' (Jones 1982: 4, 1985: 1), an intrinsic belief in the role and its function and in the world of the simulation. He is concerned more with communication in simulations than the need to represent systems, and therefore it is communications rather than the real world that matter. As long as all the elements, procedures and behaviour seem plausible (he uses the term 'professional' for behaviour: Jones 1987: 9), a fantasy scenario would do fine. This is in tune with Thatcher and Robinson (1986: 26), who prefer the phrase (which I have borrowed in this chapter) 'representation of *an actual situation*' to 'representation of *reality*'.

There is no reason to suppose that a simulation of a fantasy world is less useful than a simulation based on the real world. The interactive or decision-making skills used and developed in a science fiction scenario, whether it be a communications simulation or a mission on a computer simulation of the Star

Ship Enterprise, would be as important in terms of learning transferable skills as a simulation based on the real world.

In terms of language/communication learning, simulations in the context of this book are seen to allow participants to develop skills, and explore the effectiveness of linguistic/communicative strategies in real-world scenarios and those of potential worlds. The world of fantasy is no less relevant to the teaching of English than the real world unless it is a world without communication. But, since effectiveness is not always appropriateness, participants should be able to link their linguistic experience in the simulation to real-world environments – to the world of the court or of the public enquiry. What matters above all though, is that for the participant there is communicative reality, a belief at an 'emotional, attitudinal and behavioural' (Keen 1992: 3) level in the simulated role, environment and problem, in the motive for language use. The simulation can provide this experience uniquely, as can be seen in Chapter 6 where language in the simulation is explored.

In terms of working with a literary text one becomes concerned with the *potential* world of the author and its peculiar reality (though this is often based on the real world). Here a systems simulation based on a dynamic *model* of this 'potential reality' can be an effective tool for deconstruction in the same way it is used to deconstruct real-world systems – as in Greenblat's *Blood Money*. One can, for example, see the choices faced by characters in the system in which they function and see the powers acting on them, to gain a deeper and experiential insight into their behaviour. The development of this kind of systems simulation, along with discussion of the potential of communications simulations, for working with a literary text is described in Chapter 2 where general design principles are considered and Chapter 3 which looks specifically at the design of a simulation for a text.

2 Designing simulations for English teaching

Despite a growing number of commercial simulations becoming available on the market, many English teachers will have experienced, or know of, very few. Probably the *Trading Game*, or *Bafa Bafa*, will rank among these. Such simulations often become available in schools because of the involvement of outside agencies such as world development centres or multicultural units using these simulations to create awareness of development or multicultural issues. Teachers who know of these simulations (which they perhaps took part in during their training) will often wait until these well-known ones become relevant to their curriculum if they use them at all. In some schools, the simulation is the preserve of the staff as a kind of management training tool, and indeed this, outside of education, has been a major area of growth for the simulation, accounting for much of its success in recent years. It would not be surprising if the simulation was identified with more significance in this area. In any case, even given teacher awareness of simulations, and access to them, it is likely to be difficult to find simulations which meet the specific needs of an English curriculum at any given time.

Simulations for English teaching are on the market, though these tend to be less well-known and accessible than those I have mentioned. One commonly used simulation, or variants of it, found in English classrooms is Ken Jones' *Front Page* (which appears in Taylor and Walford 1978: ch. 8). Participants are given roles as journalists, and have to produce a front page from stories provided by the editor. Late stories come in affecting the layout and priorities of the page, forcing on the participant the professional circumstances of the newspaper journalist. I have seen television newsroom variants where video cameras have been available. In fact, Jones has had a major influence in creating awareness about simulations in English departments in schools and in moving thinking about simulations towards the area of language and communication learning. His books about simulations are perhaps better known by English teachers than actual communications simulations themselves.

The simulation is more likely to be an event than an aspect of the curriculum.

Front Page will be dragged out as *the* work on media, or as the core of work on media. It is not often that a teacher can, during an exploration of dialect or power and language, think of walking into the stock cupboard and pulling off a tailored simulation, in the way that she might with other kinds of activities which lie abundantly on the shelf.

Given this likelihood of limited availability of the right simulation material to meet the learning needs of the ongoing curriculum, it would pay to develop your own simulations. It can be an exercise which is not too difficult or time-consuming, depending on the kind of simulation you choose, and existing simulations are easy to adapt.

PART A: FIRST STEPS

There is no fixed procedure for designing simulations. Authors will have their own approaches almost as in writing any other kind of text. The best that one can do in a chapter like this is to be aware of the elements of a simulation and to explore the approaches of other authors. The next chapter takes you through a stream of consciousness in actually developing a simulation for a text, but even this experience only reflects the processes and intellectual leaps which occurred to the author on those occasions.

There are fundamentally two kinds of simulation (as described in Chapter 1) and consequent broad approaches to design, even given the individuality of each process I have just described.

As an English teacher, is your primary concern to create certain (or any) communicative situations? Would a bit of formal talk here and confrontation there be OK? If so, then probably you will be able to be quite flexible in designing your simulation. As long as your environment is credible, or as Jones (1987: 10) describes it, 'plausible and consistent', you can start from almost anywhere as one might approach writing a novel. The process can be quite organic, as long as certain essential elements, which I will come to, are there. Even if there are certain kinds of situation from the 'real world' you want your students to experience from a communicative point of view, for example the communicative behaviour of the court, or of the executive meeting, then again design may be quite organic, around certain key elements.

If you are working with a text, it is possible that you will want to model your simulation on a *system* in the text (such as slavery) to learn about that system, to explore the behaviour of characters in the text within that system, or simply to empathize with their situation. This approach is along the lines of the systems simulations described in Chapter 1, here modelled on the author's reality as opposed to a real-world system/process (though this may amount to the same thing). This approach will control your design process much more and inevitably lead to greater control of the simulation over the participants than the options above, as I explained in Chapter 1 where I made a distinction between communications simulations and systems simulations. One needs to be much more methodical in the design of systems simulations. This is usually, by far, a more time-consuming process than that for communications simulations and to the novice designer with a busy teaching schedule it will be unrealistic to do on a frequent basis. It's the kind of thing that might be developed as a one-off to be used by several teachers, perhaps cooperatively developed, or as a major classroom exercise.

Those involved in the design of *systems simulations* based on models of a reality usually (and the literature available on design is very limited) suggest some kind of sequential approach. This has been attacked by Jones (1985: ch. 1, 1987: 30) and I shall come to this shortly. The reason for this approach is that designing a simulation based on a model of reality is a research technique closer to the work of the university department than the living room of Douglas Adams. Clearly defined aims will have been set out about the research – and like any research the aims will not be very flexible. If the investigation is into the social problems experienced by unemployed people in the benefits system, one will not end up researching the difficulties of flying across the Atlantic in Concorde. The elements of the real system must be there and constructed in relationship to each other as in a research report.

The sequence for developing a systems simulation will normally go something like this:

1 *Aims and parameters*. This will involve primarily identifying an aspect of life (or a literary text) which operates in a unitary way – a system which can be extracted and made to work independently. Considerations about the context for the use of the simulation will also need to be made, including the purpose, resources and 'audience'.
2 *Developing the model of the reality*. This means working out the elements of the real system and the relationships of these to each other. This includes the people involved (roles), how they fit into the system (function), power relationships, what opportunities roles have to function (to make decisions, to act), how much power they have, and so on. Variables for the system dynamic must also be established. What would happen to one part of the system if another did this or changed in this way? If x is unemployed for so long, what will happen to x or y? If unemployment rises does benefit go down? What then happens to each role?
3 *Reproducing the elements and relationships of the model in a simulation*. This will involve adjusting the model to suit the limitations of the classroom, the number of students and perhaps further simplification of the system to make it workable, even though the model will anyway be a simplified and extracted version of the reality (as I explained in Chapter 1). It is at this point that any creativity emerges, and this is usually restricted to finding representations or metaphors for roles, actions, environment, and the overall problem (surviving

on a particular housing benefit scheme). Creativity becomes a search for puns for, or representations of, elements of the actual system, and the way the simulation is painted. What is critical is to build in decision-making stages which represent those facing the real-life participants in the given system. The dynamic of the simulation will emerge from these decisions. Rules will be required to keep the participants focused on the *required* or relevant action/ processes. These will reflect as far as possible those which exist in real life, but there will need to be some which don't necessarily exist in real life (Taylor and Walford 1978: 46) because of the artificial context in which the system is placed. The roles need to be kept exercised in terms of their relevance to the dynamic of the model or system problem, rather than as the roles might otherwise behave (for example, in other aspects of their job or in their social lives).

4 The final stage, which is likely to be an ongoing process, is *testing the simulation against the model and refining it*. Simulations never work as expected first time and never according to the model of reality.

The practical experience of working through this kind of simulation is discussed in greater depth in the next chapter, where the ideas described above are given more concrete expression.

Communications simulations, as I explained in Chapter 1, can emphasize controls (rules) and outcomes much less than systems simulations. These are often left to the self-discipline of participants using their 'existing knowledge' (Jones 1987: 31 – although this specific reference describes children's early 'doctor and patient' simulations). This is a key difference between a systems model which imposes this knowledge, often in a compressed form, and a communications simulation. If there is to be a court case, the participants will be expected to know how to behave, although some procedural codes might be included in the documentation. The author provides information, for example a problem or issue and the situation, but the ongoing dynamic is more likely to be in the form of changing forums for decision-making and gradual input of information rather than given variables for outcomes.

Jones suggests a skeleton on which to hang the design process by isolating what he sees as the four basic elements of the simulation. His definition of a simulation and the design process is very much tied to interactive/communicative simulations. He sees the process as a creative one fleshing out, in almost inspirational fashion, the meat around the four bones (Jones 1985: 17, 1987: 30):

- What is the problem?
- Who are the participants?
- What do they have to do?
- What do they do it with?

This works fine if you are concerned primarily with the interactive experiences of participants. The model, as I have just described it in relation to systems simulations, has no defining place in Jones' construction of simulations because he *is* concerned with the interaction of participants. He is neither bound by *aims* (to the same rigidity), made concrete in the model of a reality, nor by the sequence of approach. It would be viable to see the aims as the participant experiences *first*, around which the system is built rather than vice versa as above. This is why he can say, 'The actual starting point of the whole mental process need not be an aim, but an idea about the contents' (1985: 9), and later, 'If you are fascinated by any particular document ... see if the simulation can be built around it' (1985: 37). He can thus describe a much more flexible approach. Aims for him *are* flexible and secondary to the creative spirit.

It would, of course, be nonsense to suggest that in the development of the systems simulation in the next chapter my thoughts operated entirely in linear fashion. I did have moments of inspiration which I cannot account for as part of some conscious, mechanical process. On the whole, though, the process was highly structured, and my moments of 'inspiration' were framed by needs arising from a design *sequence*.

Whatever kind of simulation you choose to develop, the four essential 'ingredients' (Jones 1985: 13) described by Jones do seem to provide a useful way in – and they might also be the first step to inform your development of a research model in a systems simulation. In developing a real-world systems simulation entitled *Capjefos*, about development in an African village, Greenblat (1987: 27) developed her model around the same ideas – 'Actors' (roles), 'goals' (in relation to problem or issue), 'activities' (function) and 'resources' (tools) – within the overall problem of development:

ACTOR	GOALS	ACTIVITIES	RESOURCES
Village male farmer	increase cash crop	farming	land

She was then able to establish linkages between these elements. Indeed, this approach of breaking down the system into its component parts in this way, starting with roles or 'actors', forms the early stage of my design of the *Roll of Thunder* simulation in the next chapter.

When you begin the process it might be worth asking the following questions:

- How much time do you have?
- Would the time-consuming development of a model of a system give a value in working with a text which would outweigh that of a communications simulation? It might be more worthwhile to have a simulation along the lines of a meeting or hearing in a different scenario to that of the text to follow up incidents which actually took place in the text.
- Do you want to impose an authoritarian model on your students where *your* model is presented, or for them to create much of the model in the action?
- Do you want them to create the model as a classroom exercise?

Since the next chapter explores the development of a systems simulation in detail and includes the first steps in my thinking, I describe below how one might approach the design of a communications simulation.

If you go to your local library and open up *English Historical Documents*, on page 267 of Volume XII (2) you'll find a document called 'Royal Commission on Poorer Classes in Ireland, 1836' which is abbreviated below:

(Third Report of the Royal Commission on the Condition of the Poorer Classes in Ireland, Parliamentary Papers 1836, XXX)

(Section 1) The evidence annexed to our former reports proves to painful certainty that there is in all parts of Ireland much and deep-seated distress.

There is not in Ireland the division of labour that exists in Great Britain; the body of the labouring class look to agricultural employment, and to it only, for support; the supply of agricultural labour is thus so considerable, as greatly to exceed the demand for it; hence come, small earnings, and widespread misery . . .

It appears that in Great Britain the agricultural families constitute little more than a fourth while in Ireland they constitute about two-thirds of the whole population; that there were in Great Britain in 1831, 1,055,982 agricultural labourers, in Ireland 1,131,715, although the cultivated land of Great Britain amounts to about 34,250,000 acres and that of Ireland only to about 14,600,000.

We thus find that there are in Ireland about five agricultural labourers for every two that there are the same quantity of land in Great Britain . . .

A great proportion of them are insufficiently provided at any time with the commonest necessaries of life. Their habitations are wretched hovels, several of a family sleep together upon straw or upon the bare ground, sometimes with a blanket, sometimes even without so much to cover them; their food commonly consists of dry potatoes, and with these they are sometimes so scantily supplied as to be obliged to stint themselves to one spare meal in the day. There are even instances of persons being driven by hunger to seek sustenance in wild herbs. They sometimes get a herring, or a little milk, but they never get meat except at Christmas, Easter, and shrovetide . . .

The wives and children of many are occasionally obliged to beg; they do so reluctantly, and with shame, and in general go to a distance from home that they may not be known . . .

With these facts before us, we cannot hesitate to state that we consider remedial measures requisite to ameliorate the condition of the Irish poor.

You have, here, the basis of a simulation. From here you might think about a number of possible developments. What about an exploration of language registers and dialect? Encoded in the document are all kinds of information about language which might provide a model for participants in a simulation: the formal register, the vocabulary, the general functional appropriateness for the purpose (including audience) and the time. The students could not only explore this document, but they could use this register in their output in the simulation.

You might establish the likely *roles* involved in the background to this document. Perhaps the evidence for this document was achieved through interviews with the poor. Could a commission investigating the poor be the main function of the simulation involving writing such a report? Would this then mean having roles for the Royal Commission members, for the poor, for those more fortunate people who maybe don't wish to provide more support for the poor? Could the poor be establishing some kind of campaign, resourced in part by this document (and others that could be invented)? How would the roles come together? When? How would they all be occupied all of the time? What kind of an issue or problem can their functions revolve around? Could the commission establish an inquiry which the various role sets attend?

A *scenario* is already taking shape – the problem and the setting for the simulation. The roles are starting to emerge along with their possible functions. Perhaps *documents* could include factual information about the circumstances of the poor on which a commission could act. Documents might also include procedures for parliamentary investigation and for the compilation of parliamentary reports.

Now what about those objectives? The participants need not only to read the document but to use the language of the document in some way. What about if they have to present further written evidence to parliament? A second report. And Jones' point about consistency is going to be especially important here. The participants must be submerged in the registers of the time in the documentation they receive. A further visit to the library might enable the provision of other kinds of documents relating to the issue from the time for comparative purposes.

Debriefing points already start to become available. How does the language of the document(s) compare with similar parliamentary documents of today? How might the documents produced by the participants compare with those provided in the simulation?

This stream of consciousness shows the potential for a multitude of directions in which one's thinking could go (though one should probably argue for stronger curriculum objectives at the outset than is suggested here). Already two major scenarios have emerged – the Commission's report on the poor to parliament, or some kind of campaign by the poor. The two might not be incompatible, but it's best to keep things simple. It's best to have simple objectives for the roles and the simulation, a clear issue, and a simple set of role interactions (for and against the issue, for example) to start off with. More complicated developments might then grow out of the actual practise of the simulation.

One can start from any of the elements of a simulation. It could be a role. It could be a setting. It's much easier to start with an issue that already exists, of course, since the issue itself, the roles and their interests and powers, etc., will already be established. Local government provides an excellent structure for a simulation and issues can be resourced from the local newspaper.

Working with a literary text

Working with a literary text requires certain special considerations from the outset of the design process, which this author has become aware of through experience. In working with a text do not mimic the plot. The whole thing about any kind of simulation is that outcomes are unpredictable – even in systems simulations with heavy designer authorship. So one would *not* aim to build the structure around a sequence of events in a text where these involve decisions taken by characters, although one might use *situations* in the text for the scenario. This sounds obvious given discussion of the nature of simulations in Chapter 1, but to the novice designer, working from the plot can be a tempting way forwards – almost an obvious first step.

In the next chapter I describe in the planning of *Roll of Thunder*, that it is better, where students know the text, to have analogous situations, roles and power relationships, as opposed to actual ones from a text to avoid impersonation of and influences from the behaviour which takes place in the text. However, new roles can be invented to explore the text. At the end of the book *Roll of Thunder, Hear My Cry* (Taylor 1990), a black boy faces a trial for murder, although the circumstances are rather dubious. There is no reason why an inquiry couldn't be set up with committee members examining evidence that comes from the text in the form of documentation – a tape-recording, letters, or even participation by the controller as a witness to the events of the book.

A big temptation is to cover too much of a text when thinking about design. If one of the aims for using the simulation is to convey knowledge, one can be inclined to incorporate as much as possible. One might wish to cover the whole of the plot or all of the threads which run through the text – the social, economic, political themes and all the character relationships. It's best, at least initially, to think about a part of the text – perhaps one incident and build out from there. In working with *Roll of Thunder, Hear My Cry*, I took one key incident which was the boycotting of a white shop by members of the black community. This seemed significant and I then tied in related ideas. Try not to make the structure of the simulation too complex – complex ideas can be developed during the debrief.

Not all texts will lend themselves to systems simulations. Many will not have, or do not make explicit, definable systems (e.g. economic or social systems) in the way that *Roll of Thunder, Hear My Cry* does. If the emphasis of a text is on personality and relationships between individuals, rather than the environment in which they function, it may be difficult to build a model around this. In the real world, research can be done into any system, but if it is not there in the text, then it is difficult to define and in fact is probably of little significance to the text anyway.

If a text does not lend itself to a model, useful analysis can still be brought about through a communications simulation. For example, in a love story, a meeting between parents may take place to discuss the problems involved in a love match. The structure of the simulation itself does not have to come from the text, it could be a fiction of the simulation based on a meeting of social workers with case notes using evidence from the text. The problem need not be based on events in the text but could be a fictional problem consistent with the text: Should Mary be allowed to adopt a child? Evidence of child abuse which actually takes place in the text could be used. I found it difficult to produce a systems simulation for *Across the Barricades* (Lingard 1972), a novel in which two sets of lovers – a Catholic girl and a Protestant boy and vice versa – create tensions in both sets of families and communities. A consistent extension of this might be to have the two sets of lovers tried in a Protestant or Catholic paramilitary 'court' or for the two families to meet to try to decide whether to interfere in the relationships. Evidence presented could be drawn from the text. One can simply extract an issue or problem from a text, without having to have a systematic model, and this would still provide a framework for analysis in the debrief and follow-up work.

If you want to base your simulation on a model of a system in the text, it can be useful to design the simulation to be run before reading the text. One has the advantage here of being able to use the actual scenarios, names and other factual information of the text. In this way, the simulation can be used to develop a knowledge of the elements of the text as well as an understanding of processes that work within it. If participants have read the text, it would be necessary to develop analogous representations, as I have suggested and as in the case of *Roll of Thunder* which follows, so that participants don't mimic the known behaviour of the characters.

PART B: NUTS AND BOLTS AND BUILDING REGULATIONS

Documentation

Simulations need documentation to inform the participants of key information including their roles, other roles (where appropriate), role functions, the scenario, and the central and other problem(s). They need also to know how they are allowed to behave and what powers they have, including information relevant to accomplishing their task. Documentation can take the form of written role cards, other written or visual information which informs, including maps and police statements, and even things said or done by the controller before or during the simulation.

Intrinsic vs *extrinsic documents*

Intrinsic documents are presented within the reality of the world of the simulation. For example, in order to establish the relationship between two functional roles in the simulation, one role might receive a letter from the other. This document from the *Roll of Thunder* simulation establishes the role, some of its function and knowledge of the situation and other roles from within:

Uncle's Farm

Date: End of Year 10

To Yellow Farm

Brother Yellows

Just a note about the ginning this year. Don't forget to record how many times we have done ginning for those Reds. You forgot some last year and we lost money. Every time we do one gin, keep a record of which Red it was for in the book, as we agreed. Then we can easily work out how much they owe us at the end of the year. Don't forget – we agreed we'd charge 'em 5 Rollads every gin we do.

I see them Reds borrowed quite a lot of money from us to buy supplies from the shop. We made 16 Rollads in interest according to the accounts sheet for this year (Year 10). Tell the shopkeeper we'll still give credit this year. We'll lend the Reds money for anything they want from the shop.

I sure am unhappy with the Reds over here on uncle's land. They seem right uppity. They just don't do what they're told anymore. Think they're as good as us these days!

Let's hope they produce lots of nottocs this year, anyway. Lots of ginning for us, eh!

Your brother

The letter below serves a similar function:

North State

Date: End of Year 10

To my family

It's so different up here in North State. The Yellows up here treat us so good. I heard how badly those Yellows down your way have been treating us Reds. They're so rude and I'm sure they take more of your money than they need to.

I heard old Big Red was put on the chain gang for trying to escape without paying his debts to that Yellow blood sucker on your estate. I wish for the day when we all have a little smallholding so we aren't so dependent on the Yellows. I suppose that day's a long way off!

Well, take care now.

Your loving Annie

Extrinsic documents might have been in the form of role cards which told participants, author to student, who they were, what they had to do and so on:

You are a landowner. Your job is to gin nottocs. You must write down in a book every time you do a gin . . .

My own preference is for intrinsic documents particularly where social or communicative reality is important to the simulation.

Extrinsic documents interfere with the reality of the simulation. They are usually given to participants during the briefing before the action takes place. They create outside reference points, since participants refer to the external (classroom) world of the pre-simulation briefing during the action to define their roles and purpose from information they were given. They are also extracted from their simulation world by the extrinsic language on their documents. Such documentation detracts from the role, function and environment of the simulation.

I like to think of the intrinsic approach as something like the television series *Quantum Leap*. The lead character in this series, affected by exposure to some scientific experiment, finds himself projected backwards in time to a different period each week – but unlike most time travel fictions, he finds himself inside the skin of a person who existed at the time. In the mirror he sees himself, but others see the flesh of the character he has assumed. He can only become aware of who he is and what he does through interaction with his environment. He becomes curious and investigates, gradually adapting his behaviour to the circumstances in which he finds himself. This just wouldn't be the same if someone came up to him and said, 'Oh by the way, you're Martin Luther King!' He takes for granted the reality not only of the situation but of the other roles. They don't fumble their way uncomfortably into an 'act'.

Even though I explained in the first chapter that reality is compromised in systems simulations where there is tokenistic representation of the social situation, which makes the participant one step removed from the social/communicative reality, reflection by the reader on participation in *Monopoly* will demonstrate how important it is to have chance cards addressed to *you* rather than to a third party (like Professor Plum in *Cluedo*). Even if one is not experiencing the 'full' reality of the social situation, one is able to feel the decision-making context more empathetically, even here, with intrinsic documents.

Intrinsic documentation has the further advantage of assisting in the allocation of roles. During the briefing stage of the simulation, the allocation of roles through extrinsic role cards can lead to initial negativity and disappointment with some children. You might, for example, give a role card to one student describing her as a detective, and give another student a role card which describes her as a microbiologist. While I attribute no particular value here to either of these occupations, students might when they start to compare their role cards. A gradual *realization* of who you are within the social context of the simulation through intrinsic documents, such as the letters above, seems to avoid this. The choosing stage is avoided and it is more about 'Who am I?' than 'What have I been given?', a kind of acceptable *fait accompli*.

There are, however, occasions where it might be more appropriate to have extrinsic documents. All the necessary information may be provided by the letters to Yellow Farm or by the controller in role asking how the plantation's going (perhaps key information about the participant's job), but latching onto the meaning of information presented intrinsically in this way may prove difficult for some: 'How does this apply to me?', 'What's going on?' Extrinsic explanations by the controller, such as documents saying 'You are so and so and you have to . . .' can be easier to understand. Simulations get off to notoriously slow starts as participants define their roles and functions. The intrinsic approach which has to be 'put together' jig-saw fashion by the participant can make this more the case.

Jones (1985: 35) writes 'notes for participants' to 'explain directly to the participants what the simulation is all about, and what they can and cannot do'. These are viewed, naturally, before or at the start of the simulation. I would not be inclined to do this since, as I have explained, this creates outside reference points and may lead to less 'honest' behaviour in the simulation. Jones believes that using these notes might, for example, mean the controller doesn't have to intervene, thus breaking the reality. The problem is that participant behaviour is then controlled constantly by the pre-simulation reference to behaviour. I am much more in favour, idealistically perhaps, of making the simulation control the reality – it must work! As a last resort, one might 'police' the activity through intrinsic controllers who could advise, as 'documents', on appropriate behaviour within the world of the simulation. These need to be consistent with the reality of the simulated world in the way they are in the real world with police, teachers, courts and other social devices. These roles might be considered at the design stage, although they might more appropriately be defined according to and at the time of the problem by the controller.

There is no reason why all instructions which take place in the briefing and all role and function descriptions shouldn't be able to be made intrinsic if this is the approach you choose. This includes how to use the resources. For example, if one doesn't want people to touch technological equipment which is sensitive and vital to the simulation, one can write a document purporting to be from the computer manufacturer:

ZPC INC.

Accepts no responsibility for failure of this device due to misuse. Misuse includes . . . tampering with this machinery in operation mode.

This does require imagination and effort, and takes designer thinking a stage further than 'writing the rules'.

Materials should make the controller aware of her role where this is intrinsic. Although it may be that you as designer will also be controller, will you remember what you need to next year, or will you pass your simulation on to others to use? The line between briefing and interfering needs to be made clear. What are the parameters for the controller's behaviour? It may be that you don't want to give her much lateral movement and therefore you state things that she must say and do and make it clear that nothing else should be added. It may be that you set objectives:

> You must present the view that your organization has called the meeting to establish the cheapest way to build the tunnel with minimal environmental damage. You will chair the committee to ensure that these criteria are emphasized.

From here the controller might improvise within these clear parameters. Care is needed here though, and any possible contradictory behaviour which might damage the simulation should be made clear. This applies equally to those impromptu roles for policing the activity I mentioned above.

In a good simulation, the functions of the participants should be enough to create reality. The participants should be preoccupied with their tasks and their relationships with other elements in the simulation, including other participants, in such a focused way that other information (their classroom, the outside world) should fade from the scenario. However, the physical environment can assist in creating this alternative reality by providing anchors to it. In simulations which take place in an unfamiliar location, it is always useful to provide a map of the area – even if this is not significant to the work of the simulation (for example, even if it's not about local conservation or town planning which might be based around maps). In the simulation to be described in Chapter 6, I dress formally as a company executive and this, as a form of documentation, describes much about the social/behavioural environment of the simulation world (though these codes might not be adhered to by the participants). The significance of the environment is becoming increasingly recognized by hospitals, many of which now decorate delivery rooms as living rooms, and this is seen to have a significant effect on the feelings of parents giving birth. Dress and the environment as described here are also kinds of intrinsic documentation providing information which could be written on a role card (though this in practice would be too detailed and distracting). The environment can be significant in engaging participants in the early stages of a simulation when they have not yet defined their roles and relationships.

As with all elements of the simulation, the role and the issue, and so forth, try not to give conflicting or confusing signals about the environment. It's important for the participants to know where they are and messages about this must be consistent. More is said about intrinsic and extrinsic documentation and the role of the controller in Chapter 4, 'Running the simulation'.

Access to documents

It should be clear to the controller and the participants how to use the documents. It might be that they need to be read or seen or heard in a particular order to make sense. The controller might be required to hold some things back from the participants. Premature access to these documents might spell disaster!

If all the members of a group need to be aware of the contents of documents, explain for the controller that a copy should be given to each member of the group or include an activity which forces sharing of the information. Otherwise, some may read while others don't, or some won't be able to catch up as things move on and they will become overwhelmed. Make sure there is enough time included for the participants to see all of the documents. Try not to saturate the participants with information, as this can be a turn off or simply confusing. Gradual leakage of information and simple key information, where possible, can be better.

Make sure the documents are accessible to the participants. What will happen to those with reading difficulties in a mixed-ability class? Will all participants who need to, be able to read and understand the documents? Can you provide salient points for adaptation by the teacher running the simulation? Think about how the human documents, the roles and their functions, can be made clear to those around them. Badges, for example, can be vital in simulations with large numbers of people where confusion might otherwise prevail. There can be no better brake on the reality of a simulation than to have people wandering around asking: 'Who are you! . . . Oh sorry, I'm looking for . . .'.

As I have mentioned, some simulations, particularly those which I have described as systems simulations, require little or no prior knowledge on the part of the participant. Such knowledge is built, or documented, into the system. For example, no formal knowledge of business capitalism is required to play *Monopoly*, although some sense of capitalism, mathematics, etc., is. On the other hand, I suggested that communications simulations can rely greatly on participant knowledge. Be sure that the participants do know enough about the system being represented, including its conventions or rules, so that they will be able to function appropriately. You can't simply assume that they will know how a judge (trials are popular school simulations) behaves, or is expected to behave, or about the procedures of a union–management meeting. You might need to provide models – perhaps a video of the event to be simulated – or other guidance here. There is further development of this discussion in Chapter 6.

Roles

A key issue in simulation design is to do with the extent of control of the simulation (designer) over the participants. There was some discussion of this in Chapter 1 in making a distinction between a communications simulation, in which participants have considerable control over behavioural and decision-making options, and systems simulations based on models, in which these kinds of participant behaviour can be very limited by the designer's interpretation of the model.

One of the key learning advantages of any simulation is its ability to allow participants to *feel* and *behave* empathetically and intrinsically, as a starting point for deconstruction of either the system in which they find themselves or of their own behaviour. Once you *give* participants feelings, or make choices about decisions on their behalf, you remove this *felt* aspect of the learning and move towards pretence and caricature, removing any meaningful starting point to understanding of the situation at hand. This is not the same as limiting participants' decisions through a tightly constructed systems simulation which confines functionality rather than proxies it.

Role documentation in a simulation would not therefore *normally* incorporate personalities, feelings or instructions about what decisions to make in response to simulation stimuli. The most acceptable line that is drawn is that one creates the circumstances in which the participants behave but one doesn't tell them *how* to behave. Simulations which use the names of characters from real life (or in the context of this book, from the literary text) externalize the behaviour of the participants as much as if they had been told how to feel or behave. They are going to ask 'How would so and so behave?' as opposed to simply behaving. They are then unlikely to appreciate in any meaningful or intrinsic sense either the emotional experience or the context for decision-making processes. One is likely to be left with caricature and unfelt experience.

Simulations which use role cards are more susceptible to allocation of feelings and guidance about behaviour than those which use intrinsic documentation. It's very easy, once you start to say 'You are Police Chief Smith' to then go on to say 'You are angry at this' or 'You disagree with that'. With intrinsic documents this is less likely, since if the controller in role, or other documents (such as the letters near the start of this chapter), suggest these things to you, you will see them within the context of the simulation world and be more likely to evaluate and reject or accept them accordingly. This point is developed further in my analysis of the *Roll of Thunder* simulation in Chapter 3 with specific reference to the two letters.

There may be occasions when one *does* want to allocate personality, and this is why I suggested above that one *normally* wouldn't do this. If one adopts the role of a judge in a simulation, one has to refer to how a judge might behave. One adopts a professional persona. Is it not just as valid to attribute a character from a book to a participant in a simulation based on a text? Could participants, having read the book, not behave 'professionally' or consistently in character role with what they know of the character? In both cases, one is attributing behaviour. There is the risk of caricature, but this also exists with the adoption of the role of, for example, a police officer ('Ev'nin' all'). This is controversial, and I'm sure would be beyond the definition of a simulation to many in the field (this contradicts my own definition in Chapter 1). It is likely to be described as 'role play' as opposed to a simulation. Such an approach might still exist within a simulated structure not replicating the plot or events of a text. A character from a book could take part in a simulation which has nothing to do with the text – Lady Chatterley in a simulation on the homeless, for example. I'm sure there could be plenty of useful analysis here in the debrief with regard to consistency of attitude and behaviour. If it suits your purpose, do it rather than be constrained by the simulation label. If you disagree, at least you will have thought through the reasons why.

This argument suggests that there is going to be some difficulty in drawing the line between creating the circumstances for behaviour and not interfering in this behaviour. There are going to be behavioural expectations, particularly where there is participant discretion regarding this as in communications simulations. If a role is that of a judge, it comes with certain preconditions about not only behaviour, but emotional/value orientations which make one believe in the rule of law. Systems simulations often use explicit rules about allowed actions which take this issue away. The issue for the designer is thus not at all clear-cut but *at which point* to concede control of behaviour.

It may be that one wants to control a role to encourage a certain type of behaviour in the simulation by giving it a history of behaviour in its documentation, rather than stating directly how the role *should* behave. For example, a document might say 'You have supported this action (group) in the past'. This for me is too manipulative and bestows behaviour on the participant too artificially, even though in a sense one does this in giving functional roles in the first place as I have explained. If one wants to create a past for a role, then it is best done through a 'pre-simulation', or prior round, in which you might, for example, create the circumstances for hostility between two groups, or identification with another, on which you wish to base later interaction in the simulation. A's might be oppressed by B's in Round One and then they debate the issue or interact otherwise in Round Two. This takes time, however, and the outcomes of the 'pre-simulation' may not be as expected – this is one of the key things about simulations.

Be clear about what the function of a role is and be sure that the participant knows. This must be either explicitly stated or made clear in the relationship between what the participant knows about herself and the issue – for example, between a conservationist and a proposal to build a motorway through an environmentally sensitive area. You must really enter the participant's mind and try to eliminate the possible alternatives for action which are not relevant for that role in relation to the problem.

Related to this point about definition of function is a common problem which occurs where there are group roles (a group of participants doing the same job without being distinguished from each other) rather than specific individual roles and members of a group can be left out. This can happen, for example, where there are friendship groups within a role set who may work closely together isolating the outsider who was allocated to that group. It can be useful to create individual roles within the role set so that all members of the group have to function for the set to achieve their objectives. As designer, of course, one cannot predict the numbers who will be taking part on the day and it may be that to an extent this will have to be left for the controller to sort out (see Chapter 4). I think it could be argued that where a simulation is powerful enough and where belief in the function of the role and the motivation are strong enough, undifferentiated roles within a role set will work. The *Trading Game*, which simulates production and trading patterns between what might be described as the 'Southern and Northern hemisphere' countries, based on inequality of resources, never fails to achieve intensive group cooperation. These role sets are left to sort out their own organization.

Structure

A simulation will take place over rounds or 'pulses' during which decisions are made in response to stimuli. A communications simulation may only have one round – a debate or meeting, for example. *Monopoly*, for example, has its many rounds defined by circuits of the board. The end of a round may include an accounting system which then sets up the circumstances for the next round. In Greenblat's *Blood Money*, employers learn from the first round that it might not be wise to employ haemophiliacs who are unreliable. The second round might thus be influenced by taking stock of the first in this way. In the *Roll of Thunder* simulation described in the next chapter, sharecroppers and landowners take stock at the end of each round (representing a year) of their finances and credit and debt relationship to each other and formulate decisions about how to organize the following year's activities. A communications simulation may have a first round which allows interest groups to establish their point of view on an issue before then taking part in a debate or meeting with other interest groups.

Each round will need to have a clear problem focus which ties in with the overall problem of the simulation. Set sustainable problems. Break a complex problem into smaller, achievable units. Try to provide ongoing stimulus during the simulation rather than just setting up a round and leaving participants to it for an hour. Bleed documentation into the simulation, providing ongoing stimulus about the issue or problem. The appearance of messages or news stories (in Jones' *Front Page*, for example; see Taylor and Walford 1978: ch. 8) excites the participants and maintains focus.

Set time limits and deadlines for activities or find some way of allowing the participants to bring activities to an end when appropriate. You will usually have to make sure that different role sets complete their tasks at the same time – otherwise some wait around, bored and removing themselves from the reality of the simulation world while others need more time. Timing is the element most likely to need adjustment after the first run. In the *Roll of Thunder* simulation I had one set of participants (the sharecroppers) manufacturing an item ('nottocs') which then had to be processed by another set of participants (the landowners). I expected each nottoc to be manufactured and ready for processing in a matter of thirty seconds or so; instead, they took several minutes, leaving the landowners with nothing to do. I had to change the criteria (intrinsically in the role of trader), lowering the quality, and thus the production time, of the nottocs, explaining this in terms of a market shortage of the product allowing inferior quality to be accepted, to get the dynamic going again.

If the simulation needs to run its full course, you must be careful in design to make sure that key decisions or behaviour don't occur at points, like the end of an early round, where they may terminate the simulation. For example, in a systems-type simulation on racism, the first round might be designed to create different points of view from different role sets. You may then wish to throw these different role sets into the same arena in a second round which depends on conflict. Supposing the two (or more) groups make a decision in the first round that will not let them come into conflict in the second? Their final comment may be, 'We don't want to exploit the green people', and yet the second round may have depended on this. If your simulation uses money, it may be that a second round can only work if roles have money to take part. What happens if they go into debt at the end of the first round?

It is important to ensure continuity of roles from one round to the next. You can't have a role which is key in one round and then becomes redundant in a later round simply to serve your structure. What are participants going to do when their roles are no longer functional? Role switching is dodgy (unless a new follow-up simulation in which all roles are new is taking place) – it is confusing and breaks the reality for the participant concerned and for those around her who have come to identify a particular functional relationship with that person.

Participants must know what the structure of the simulation is – that is the fabric which cannot be interfered with. They must know the difference between painting a living room and demolishing a stress-bearing wall. To a degree, participants are going to invent aspects of the simulation, whether this be aspects of their role, their relationship with other roles or with their environment. They will have to do this to make sense of their identity, using key clues about themselves which are provided. It must be made clear to the participants which aspects of the simulation they can invent and which they cannot. I once started as a participant in a simulation where I was given certain information about my role in relation to the central problem of the simulation and how I was related to others. Other roles seemed to have occupations – information which I was not given initially. I therefore invented for myself the role of businessperson who had made his fortune selling jokes (I had one or two with me which I felt I could use legitimately in connection with my occupation in the simulation). Having left a dog 'turd' on the carpet next to the bottom of the controller's dog (it was at their house) and celebrated my meteoric rise in the jokes industry with other participants, I discovered in a later round that I was a 'respectable' publisher and that this occupation was quite crucial to the activity! In a drama, or other kind of role activity, these developments would be quite acceptable. In a simulation the relationships of the *functions* of roles to each other and to the problem *need* to be maintained, otherwise one introduces conflict of purpose, confusion, the end of both reality and the dynamic of the simulation. In this case, other roles had their functions defined by my presence as a publisher in the simulation. Maintaining the balance or tension between author structure and participant fiction is one of the most difficult aspects of simulation writing.

Access to all the information that participants must have for them to function in relation to the problem and thus for the simulation to function must be ensured in developing the structure of the simulation (unless failure to do so is an intended possibility). I have attended a 'murder' dinner which was designed for a small informal group of six persons. The dinner had several rounds: during each round certain participants would be given information about the murder which either they could release according to questioning by others or which they had to throw into the situation. The forum for sharing the information (the dinner table) was intended to ensure that information given was public domain, i.e. the knowledge would be shared with all present. The idea was adapted for a much larger group of about fourteen. During each information sharing stage people gathered away from the dinner table, in pairs or small groups, since this was the only manageable way for people to interact, and by the end of each round it was a matter of chance as to whether key information had reached people according to how far each participant had progressed through intimate conversations with the large number of people present. The structure denied the opportunity for participants to gather enough evidence to make an informed judgement. I'm not sure whether I would describe the activity as a simulation, incidentally, since behaviour was dictated and in real life there would be no *right* answer as is given at the end here – only the consensus (or otherwise) of those present. The point transfers well to simulations, however.

In the later stages of design, run through the simulation from the perspective of each role set to make sure there are no (likely) gaps in receiving necessary input from other participants or the controller or other mechanisms, and also that each role set is able to participate in appropriate decision-making stages. Thinking this through is not very different from working out the situation of each student in other kinds of lesson planning.

3 Designing a simulation: *Roll of Thunder*

First steps

What follows is an account of the thought processes of the author in developing a simulation based on Mildred D. Taylor's (1990) *Roll of Thunder, Hear My Cry*. This is not a guide to simulation design, since there is no one route to the final simulation. It does, I hope, provide an insight into some of the processes, possibilities and restrictions involved.

The book describes life in Mississippi in the 1930s for a black girl, Cassie, her family and her sharecropping community within the context of racial oppression. The book accompanies Cassie through a growing realization of the systematic nature of the racial prejudice and oppression which surrounds her. Racism is expressed through violence, which finds institutional tolerance, and is enforced through the economic power which some white members of the community have over the black members. This power strikes at the very survival of the black community and consequently creates an inability to respond to the tragic inequalities and injustices they experience.

The simulation was developed to be used with a group of 14- to 15-year-olds (Year 10). The group had read the text during the spring term and the simulation was run near the beginning of the following term. This, of course, was to be important to the design of the simulation, as I suggested in the last chapter, since the students were familiar with the events and factual information relating to the text and with the behavioural characteristics of the characters.

The simulation was developed for the purpose of inclusion in this book and naturally at the same time to be of use to the students with whom I would be working. I recorded developments as I worked on the simulation and the account below is based on this kind of stream of consciousness. The account includes ideas that occurred and were rejected as well as those which finally ended up in the simulation, to show the kinds of options that might be available at given points in the development.

I worked within a time limit of about two weeks, having already read the text, and I was still working on the simulation well into the night before it was run. This forced me into unsatisfactory compromises. I have included these and other warts for discussion, since it is likely that these kinds of compromises and failures will occur for other simulation authors. Like the simulation itself, it is from failure as well as from success that we learn. It is my intention that something of the reality and practicality of producing a simulation while under pressure (in many cases this will be alongside a teaching schedule) will come through.

My thinking was framed initially by two key questions:

1 What do I want to get out of the text?
2 What kind of a simulation do I want to use? That is, do I want to develop a systems simulation or a communications simulation (see Chapters 1 and 2 for definitions)?

I found myself first counterpoising these two questions rather than being able to answer one and then the other. The kind of simulation would depend very much on what the text could support. It would be no good attempting a systems simulation if there was no system to be modelled. Equally, the simulation might dictate what I would be able to get out of the text. In fact, as I shall describe, there were certain things I would like to have included which were marginalized and excluded by the structure of the simulation I eventually adopted. I was troubled by the degree to which the simulation structure might control my thinking as opposed to what I simply would like to have explored in the text.

With regard to the second question, I had to consider wider educational and practical issues. Did I want to impose *my* model, or analysis, of the text if a model could be developed from *Roll of Thunder*? Could I afford the time to do the research, develop the model and translate this into a simulation? Would a more open simulation such as a communications simulation give participants more opportunity to bring *their* knowledge of the text to the simulation, since they had read the text? This would seem to be a less authoritarian approach, although in either case deconstruction of the simulation structure during the debrief would allow whichever simulation was chosen to be challenged. Certainly a communications simulation would be quicker to write.

Bearing in mind these questions, I began to focus on what seemed to me to be the key theme of the book; the system of white oppression of black people and the actual and potential scope for black resistance. The first thing I did was to identify the characters who were in some functional way involved in the oppression. At this point I hadn't identified a system as such, although I was aware of some relationships (who was exploiting who). I simply plotted on a piece of paper those who oppressed, those who *were* oppressed and any others who impinged on these relationships. By each character I noted how they fitted into this theme; that is, what they did, who they related to and by implication what powers or resources they had, all in terms of the oppression. In simplified form, my notes started to look something like this:

Oppressors

White Landowner

Rents land to sharecroppers
Gins (processes) sharecroppers' and smallholders' cotton
Gives credit to those who buy from the store

White Store Owners

Sell supplies to sharecroppers/smallholders to subsist and grow cotton
Give credit on behalf of landowner

....

Oppressed

Black Sharecroppers

Grow cotton
Pay landowner for ginning cotton
Buy supplies at shop
Sell cotton (through landowner)
Rent land from landowner

Black Smallholders

Grow cotton
Pay landowner for ginning cotton
Buy supplies at shop
Sell cotton
(Own own land)

My notes at this point were actually littered with examples of racial injustice. On the same sheet I had examples such as the white school having more books and buses than the black school and Cassie being served after white customers in a white shop. These were all part of a systematic oppression of the black people. But taking shape on my paper was what seemed to be a system of its own, which could work in a dynamic, unitary way, of which these incidents were not a part. I could have chosen to keep all my records of racial incidents. Perhaps I could have simulated a meeting to discuss rebellion. Participants could have brought anything relevant to the simulation (or I could have included these in my documents), such as incidents of injustice, or information about the kinds of power the black community had to rebel with or the white community had to resist. But I chose to follow up the relationships which revolved around the economic system of sharecropping as indicated in the notes above. This is where the power really lay for the white racist community and this had been the crux, in the book, of the failure of the black community to respond. The functions above the dotted line in my notes, in the book at least, controlled those under the line. I started to pen in the dynamics of the relationships in diagrammatic form, although this is presented for reasons of intelligibility in textual form here. My own thinking found it easier to look at the dynamics from each role perspective rather than through an overview:

1 *(The powerlessness of) the black sharecropper.* Starts off in debt. Has to borrow from the landowner to buy supplies at the store to eat and produce cotton, to pay rent to the landowner (on whose land they live and work) and to pay the landowner for ginning cotton (both in kind as a percentage of the cotton crop). Interest on loans leads to a growing debt trap. The land resource is always inadequate to earn enough to repay the debt. The store overcharges, further increasing the debt, but the sharecropper cannot go elsewhere because the landowner will only back credit at the local store. In sum, debt enslaves the black sharecroppers.
2 *The smallholders.* Start off with a small amount of money. They don't pay rent (the smallholders in the book have a mortgage on part of their property). They produce enough to cover the costs of ginning and supplies because of this and the size of their smallholding. Therefore they don't enter the credit debt trap. They buy from the store but have the power (money and resources) to go elsewhere.
3 *The landowner.* Can charge whatever rent, credit rates and ginning fees will produce a profit or is otherwise desirable. He (as it is in the book) can use this economic power to control the behaviour of the sharecroppers and enforce their loyalty to the local store by giving credit for only this store and by threatening to raise these charges.
4 *The storekeeper.* Can overcharge given loyalty of landowner, since sharecroppers require his credit.

In the book the smallholding family, the Logans, try to arrange a black boycott of the local store because of the overcharging and particularly because the store owners had been violent towards members of the black community. While it was comparatively easy for the Logans to carry through the boycott, the sharecroppers, trapped by the economic system in which they found themselves, found this less easy as the landowners threatened to raise rents and ginning charges, thus forcing them to buy at the local (Wallace) store. I wanted to place the students within this dynamic to understand what it was that made resistance by the black sharecroppers so difficult and to draw out the distinction between the Logans and the other sharecroppers.

It became clear that *Roll of Thunder* offered a viable 'substantive' (to borrow Greenblat's 1987: 25 term) system and that this system was core to the themes of the text. In other words, a systems simulation would be a valid approach. My concern was not with how the students would perform within a social/ communications simulation – I was not concerned with language development – but how they might analyse the system itself.

Having decided upon the systems model, I had to be quite rigorous now in excluding all the factors relating to black oppression which were not relevant, such as the inequality of school resources I have mentioned. It was difficult to find the cut-off point. All the elements had to interlink in a dynamic and *causal* set of relationships such as I have described above. It was very tempting, in anticipating possible behaviour in the simulation, to include those who attended the poor black school as people who might want to take part in a boycott, since this seemed a likely course of action as in the text – but the school issue had a separate dynamic even if it was a related issue. The issues and roles of these related elements would have floated meaninglessly on the periphery of the main action, finding no point at which to interact. It is essential to establish a *substantive* set of relationships in a dynamic model.

In a communications simulation of the kind I have mentioned, in which the dynamic is not predefined, there would be more freedom to include simply relevant information. System models give less freedom because there have to be causational linkages for them to work – everything has to have an effect on, or be affected by, something else. So whereas having no school books if you were black was highly relevant to the system of oppression, it could not fit into the dynamic of the substantive system of economic blackmail. A sharecropper meeting to discuss rebellion, however, in which incidents of oppression might be presented as evidence, would include any *relevant* or *related* information. A system does not choose an issue or problem but gives rise to them. A communications simulation focuses on one central problem or issue.

It is worth mentioning that at this stage I considered a gaming simulation to get the participants to understand the system of oppression. I could have used dice and a board or some other gaming structure. I thought I might then move into a communications simulation for the second round, so that having understood how the oppression worked first hand, they would then make a decision about whether to have a boycott in the second round, at some kind of meeting. I gave this up as a bad idea since students would have to go from being game participants to simulation participants and there would be a shift in perspective. There would be no continuity but there would be constant reference in any kind of debate to that 'outside' experience of the game. I decided to have a systems simulation, with intrinsic roles, which would take place over a number of rounds representing the year-by-year dynamic of the actual situation.

Writing the simulation

Given that the students were already familiar with the book, the first thing I did was to find metaphors for its elements and to analogize the system so that the participants wouldn't mimic or caricature the behaviour of the characters in the text. I wanted them to internalize feelings which they wouldn't do if they were 'playing' a character. They could then relate more meaningfully to the environment, behaviour and feelings of the characters. The roles were still quite recognizable but with the omission of names and race. I kept the functional roles and relationships of landowner, shopkeeper, sharecropper (represented as 'tenant' in the simulation) and smallholder. The functions were changed a little more. I used the obvious device of the alternative colours of red and yellow to replace the black and white communities, respectively. The functions, resources and relationships were translated as follows.

The smallholders and tenants made 'nottocs'. These were odd shapes drawn around a stencil which they were provided with. The shapes had to be cut out and coloured in a particular way. These had then to be taken in batches to the landowner for ginning (this term was not changed), which in the simulation was a way of bonding the nottocs together, before selling them to the controller (the market). The smallholders and tenants had to pay the landowner for ginning at the end of the year.

The smallholders and tenants had to get supplies of coloured pencils, paper and scissors to support their work from the yellow shop, although they were given an initial supply. If they had no cash for purchases, they would be given credit to be repaid with interest to the landowner at the end of the year along with other debts also subject to interest.

I hoped that the distinction between smallholder and tenant (sharecropper) as I described it earlier, might come into play for comparison with the text in the debrief (in fact this became a significant part of the later discussions). Tenants were distinguished from smallholders in the simulation in that smallholders did not pay rent at the end of the year while the tenants did, and smallholders were given a better initial supply of resources, including better tools (scissors which actually worked!), more paper and a small amount of cash which tenants did not receive, representing the greater share of land and wealth they had in the text giving them greater earning potential and thus more economic independence. The only tie with the landowner for the smallholders was the ginning fee. Would the smallholders support the tenants? Would the tenants resent the smallholders? If students could distinguish between the behaviour and responses of members of the same group to the issue in the debrief a high level of response about the issue would have been achieved. (The debrief is discussed in Chapter 5.)

The boycott which took place in the text was enabled by the existence of:

1 An alternative store free of links with the landowner (and thus not patronized by him and having to reject the boycotters) and which was prepared to trade with the black community. The store in the book is in another locality.
2 The existence of a creditor who was willing to back the purchase debts of the boycotters at the alternative store. In the book, this is a non-racist member of the white community bold enough to stand up to the social attitudes of those around him.

These elements were incorporated into the simulation as follows. The simulation starts at the end of Year 10 (simulation, not school years) and the first round is Year 11. The alternative shop comes into existence in the second round (Year 12). The shopkeepers would spend the first round living among and working as tenants so that they were empathetically placed before taking control of the shop in the second round. This solved the problem of what to do with them during the first round. From the second round, having experienced the first (or more), tenants and smallholders could make choices about buying supplies from the usual (yellow) store or going to the new (red) one.

As well as being bound by the economic hold of the white landowner in the text, the alternative store which provided the opportunity for boycott was extremely inconvenient. It was a day's travel away, meaning the loss of a day's labour, and a difficult journey. This was an important factor in contributing to the weakness of the black community in resisting the power of the landowner. This was built into the system as a long wait for those that chose to use the alternative store – about half of the productive time of each round. It was both boring for the participant making the 'journey' and meant that less nottocs could be produced.

Credit was to be provided by the controller who occupied a broad role as wholesaler, buyer and generous creditor.

The way the system in the text operated depended not just on the economic mechanics which I have described, but also on the ideological motivation (racism) of the characters who exploited the black community through these mechanics. The oppressive operation of the system was not just competitiveness, but rooted in the personae of the characters and in the community through a specific sociocultural history and socialization. This point is specifically referred to in the text by the sympathetic white lawyer, Mr Jamison, who puts up the credit for the boycotters. He explains how Harlan Granger, the landowner who finances the system of economic oppression, was indoctrinated by his grandmother (Taylor 1990: 123):

> Ever since we were boys, Harlan's lived in the past. His grandmother filled him with all kinds of tales about the glory of the South before the war. You know, back then the Grangers had one of the biggest plantations in the state and Spokane County practically belonged to them . . . and they thought it did too. They were consulted about everything concerning this area and they felt it was up to them to see that things worked smoothly, according to the law – a law basically for whites.

Indeed, the operation of the system is seen by its victims as a racial problem as Avery, one of the black sharecroppers, says (ibid.: p. 50): 'Anytime they thinks we steppin' outa our *place*, they feels they gotta stop us'. I could not hope to achieve this deep-rootedness or complexity of attitude in the white (yellow) population in the simulation.

Equally I could not motivate, or create the circumstances to motivate, the boycotters as they were motivated in the text. They were not motivated solely by material exploitation in the credit system but also, as I have said, by actual violence. It was in fact one particular incident which broke the camel's back – the burning of members of a black family accused of 'flirting' with a white girl (ibid.: p. 34). I had thought of introducing this element through the playing of a tape made by the wife of one of the victims of the burning, to try and arouse the emotional intensity of, if not empathy with, the potential boycotters. This would have been an attempt to overcome the oversimplification of this being simply an economic system when the social factors were so important. I couldn't be sure that this would compensate enough, however, since:

1 The boycotters knew the family who suffered the burnings and thus were motivated by anger over a deeply personal tragedy. The participants didn't 'know' the family who might be referred to in a tape.
2 The boycotters were themselves by implication under threat of such violence and this contributed to their motivation to react through the boycott. I could not expect the same force of motivation in a simulation since the students could never feel threatened with this violence.

I opted in the end to go ahead with the economic model. At the stage where this decision was made, I considered that it would have been too unfaithful to try to replicate these other social circumstances and excluded them (although as I describe later in this chapter, I did make unsuccessful token attempts to replicate the social circumstances at a later stage). Any differences would be ironed out in the debrief and I felt contrast or gaps would provide just as useful a framework for discussion as a more compatible system. In fact in the debrief of the simulation this was exactly what happened.

As I have indicated, the simulation took place over several rounds, each round representing a year. The simulation started at the end of Year 10. It was anticipated that participants would work out their powers in the early rounds and exercise them in the later rounds.

The accounting system was designed to create an awareness on behalf of all participants of the cycle of economic events which leads to a poverty and power trap for the sharecroppers (tenants in the simulation). All participants kept a record of accounts and the landowner fed back, at the end of each round, any debts to the tenants and smallholders if they had borrowed to pay for their ginning or to buy supplies from the shop and what interest was owed. This accounting process was designed to have considerable emphasis – perhaps five to ten minutes of filling in the accounts sheets provided – so that the implications of the power relationship would not be subsumed by the more specific activity of making things.

There had to be a starting point and so the participants were provided with completed accounts sheets for Year 10, the year previous to starting. These are shown on p. 52, 54, 57–8. These reflected more or less the kind of situation in which the characters in the text might have found themselves, in terms of the previous year's expenditure, earnings and the balance of debt or credit at the current time. Participants inherited a notional circumstance. Blank accounts sheets were then provided for Years 11, 12 and so on, according to the number of rounds which were to take place, for the participants to complete and take stock as the simulation progressed.

Landowners were free to determine their own rates of interest, rents and ginning fees from Year 11. Presumably, if these were too high, the tenants and smallholders might choose to stop work thus forcing lower rates. They might simply choose to accumulate a paper debt which is what would happen in actuality. Both the landowners and tenants would need to define the limits of their power.

Skimming the documents

For my own benefit, both during the design stage and as controller of the simulation, I produced a grid which identified who did what and when. During the design stage, the document also said what resources each role set would have, although by the time I came to run the simulation, these were explained on the Controller's notes (see pp. 63–4). In simplified form the document, which was not public domain, was much like the following:

Role	*Round 1*		*Round 2*	*Rounds 3, 4, 5 . . .*
Yellow Landowner	Ginning (Keep record of gins)	Meet with shopkeeper to assess credit Do accounts Notify and collect debts Notify new rates (if any)	As Round 1	
Yellow Shopkeeper	Buy from wholesaler Sell to tenants/ smallholders (Keep record of sales and credit)	Do accounts Notify landowner of credit sales	As Round 1	
Red Tenant	Buy resources from yellow shop Make nottocs Gin nottocs Sell nottocs to wholesaler	Do accounts Pay debts to landowner	Buy resources from yellow *or* red shop Make nottocs Gin nottocs Sell nottocs to wholesaler	
Red Smallholder	As above	As above	As above	
Red Shopkeeper	(Red tenants)	(Red tenants)	Comes into existence Buys from wholesaler Sells to tenants and smallholders	
Controller Give out resources	Sell wholesale Buy nottocs		Resources to red shop (including fly sheets to notify opening) Sell wholesale Buy nottocs	

To help understand the environment, I provided a map of the area (see p. 61) for each role set. I also provided badges describing the participants' roles, which may have detracted from reality but avoided utter confusion. The tables at which participants worked were clearly labelled 'Yellow Store', etc. The map shows the importance of spacial arrangements. There was likely to be communication between the tenants and the smallholder but not between the reds and yellows except for necessary business links. This reflected the social and physical geography of the text.

All of the documents were designed to explain the tasks clearly. Any lack of clarity might cause confusion and stop the action. 'How to gin', for example (see p. 55), explains exactly where to punch the hole so that participants don't have to ask 'Where do I make the hole?' The sheet which describes 'How to make and sell nottocs' (see p. 51) similarly tries to pre-empt the kind of detail which may lead to confusion.

I tried to make the documents intrinsic although time was not on my side. I did in fact introduce the simulation extrinsically – this was simply because I didn't have time to incorporate the briefing in intrinsic documentation. You can see this in the 'Controller's notes' (see pp. 62–4). The start and end of each round, or Year, was similarly handled extrinsically by simply declaring something to the effect of 'Year x has ended. Stop work (what you're doing). Now do the accounts'. This did feel uncomfortable and abrupt and seriously interfered with the reality. I would now build in a more intrinsic and integral mechanism to draw the year to a close, perhaps through a controller role such as a tax officer demanding accounts. I regret the sheets 'At the end of the year' (pp. 53, 59, 60), which was rushed and had to be included as an extrinsic document and equally the 'How to . . .' sheets. These could easily have been framed in an intrinsic document, 'Macallaster's Guide to Nottoc Ginning', a brief guide costing only 3 rollads! (with a cover and author attribution of course!)

The accounts sheets (pp. 52, 54, 57, 58, 60) were presented as intrinsic documents. This documentation looks 'professional' and is designed to sustain realism. A scrap of paper would not have the same effect or impose professional expectations. The document also made the task structured so that all students could accomplish it.

The letters received by the landowners (p. 56), tenants (p. 53) and smallholders (p. 53) were an intrinsic way of giving information. I preferred to have these than documents from the author explaining the task for reasons I described in the last chapter relating to the reality of the simulation.

The intrinsic nature of the documents also had a bearing on controlling participant behaviour. The letters to the landowners were designed to try and recreate the racist attitudes that prevailed in the text on the part of the white landowners (this is the token attempt at recreating the social environment I referred to earlier in this chapter). The language implicitly attributes attitude as well as the behaviour it describes. There are also indicators about what the system holds for the landowners – lots of ginning must be good. Likewise the letter to the red community sets the attitudinal and social context of the wider social group. I was not, because the documents were intrinsic, telling the participants how to behave, but I was establishing a code of expectation in the environment, no more so than might exist in the socio-economic system being simulated.

The controller's sheet, designed for myself to use on that particular day, and probably the last item to be written over breakfast, describes choosing participants for roles. This can be controversial. The mathematics involved in completing the accounts sheets could have been quite intimidating and the simulation would have been severely interrupted if this aspect failed at the end of each round. This is why the Controller's notes show role allocation of a mathematician to each group. They also suggest 'strong' people for the yellow roles. I anticipated that these roles would be the object of considerable pressure (hostility) and that they therefore had to be selected carefully. It could reasonably be argued that one should put people through things they do find difficult so that they can learn to cope with them. On this one-off occasion, this ideal was sacrificed in favour of other objectives, including completing the simulation.

The documents

I should emphasize that this is not a finished product. The simulation needs adjustments, particularly as I describe near the end of this chapter.

THE RED TENANTS

How to make and sell nottocs

Nottocs must be made at your table!

Take the stencil which looks like this:

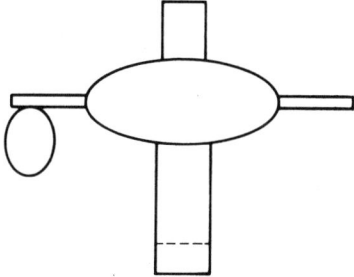

Draw round the stencil.

Draw in the missing lines.

Cut out the shape you have drawn.

Colour in the different parts of the shape with **3** colours. The **whole** shape must be coloured and the same colour must not be touching (i.e. red must not be next to red and so on).

The cutting out and the colouring must be done very carefully.

When you are satisfied with the quality of your work, take your nottocs in batches of **10** to the ginner at the 'yellow house and gin' on your map. The ginner will gin your nottocs and give them back to you. The ginner will also put the charge for the ginning on your bill and you will be expected to pay this at the end of the year.

Then take your ginned nottocs to the wholesaler. If the quality is good you will be offered a price for them.

You can get supplies of pencils, paper and scissors at the shop.

Tenants' accounts for Year 10 (11,12, etc.)

Money owed to landowner

Debt from last year	.............rollads
Table rent	.............rollads
Ginning fees	.............rollads (.....gins at .....each)
Money borrowed for shop supplies	.............rollads
Interest on money borrowed	.............rollads
	————
Total owing to landowner	.............rollads
Earnings from nottoc sales	.............rollads
Balance (take box 1 from box 2)	.............rollads credit/owed to landowner* * (delete as appropriate)

Tenants' accounts sheets are already completed for Year 10 in accordance with the figures on the 'Landowner's accounts for Year 10' (p. 57). Year 11 (the point at which the simulation starts) has only the first row ('Debt from last year') completed. The rest is completed according to progress in the simulation. Sheets for subsequent years are, of course, left uncompleted.

Everyone

I got a letter from my cousin Annie. Thought you all might like to have a copy – got it typed up specially.

Come over to the smallholding and see us sometime.

Jones and the family.

North State

Date: End of Year 10

To my family

It's so different up here in North State. The Yellows up here treat us so good. I heard how badly those Yellows down your way have been treating us Reds. They're so rude and I'm sure they take more of your money than they need to.

I heard old Big Red was put on the chain gang for trying to escape without paying his debts to that Yellow blood sucker on your estate. I wish for the day when we all have a little smallholding so we aren't so dependent on the Yellows. I suppose that day's a long way off!

Well, take care now.

Your loving Annie.

At the end of the year . . .

Fill in your accounts sheet. You may have to wait for bills to arrive from the landowner and the shop before you can do this.

You will then be expected to pay your bills if you can.

Make any decisions you need to about how you will manage next year. Will you change anything?

THE RED SMALLHOLDERS

The smallholders receive the same documents as the tenants except for the accounts sheet.

Smallholders' accounts for Year 10 (11, 12, etc.)

Money owed to landowner

Debt from last year	.............rollads
Ginning fees	.............rollads (.....gins at .....each)
Money borrowed for shop supplies	.............rollads
Interest on money borrowed	.............rollads
Total owing to landowner	.............rollads

Money spent at shop	.............rollads

Earnings from nottoc sales	.............rollads
Money left from last year	.............rollads
Total for box	.............rollads

Balance (take box 1 from box 2)	.............rollads credit/owed to landowner* * (delete as appropriate)

Tenants pay 'table rent' and this is reflected on their accounts sheet. Provision is also made on this sheet for smallholders to be in credit. As with the tenants, smallholders' accounts sheets are already completed for Year 10 in accordance with the figures on the 'Landowner's accounts for Year 10' (p. 57). Year 11 (the point at which the simulation starts) has 'Debt from last year' and 'Money left from last year' completed. Sheets for subsequent years are, of course, left uncompleted.

THE YELLOW LANDOWNERS

How to gin

This is a **nottoc**.

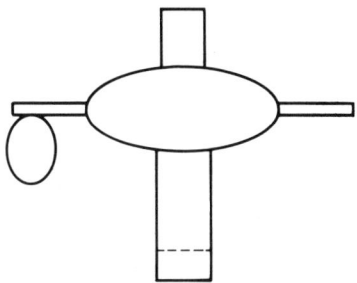

Place 10 nottocs together one on top of the other.

Fold over the bottom.

Punch through the middle with the **ginner**.

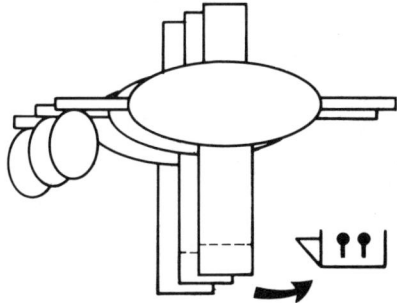

Fill in the record sheet to show whose nottocs you have ginned and how many. For example:

Person   *Amount*

Tenant 1

Tenant 2

etc . . .

Landowners also get a 'ginner', which is a form of stapler used for bonding paper without staples. It looks a little more 'industrial' than a stapler and ensures that personal staplers are not used!

Nottoc record sheet

Person	Amount
Tenant 1	....
Tenant 2	....
Tenant 3	....
Tenant 4	....
Smallholder	....

Uncle's Farm

Date: End of Year 10

To Yellow Farm

Brother Yellows

Just a note about the ginning this year. Don't forget to record how many times we have done ginning for those Reds. You forgot some last year and we lost money. Every time we do one gin, keep a record of which Red it was for in the book, as we agreed. Then we can easily work out how much they owe us at the end of the year. Don't forget – we agreed we'd charge 'em 5 Rollads every gin we do.

I see them Reds borrowed quite a lot of money from us to buy supplies from the shop. We made 16 rollads in interest according to the accounts sheet for this year (Year 10). Tell the shopkeeper we'll still give credit this year. We'll lend the Reds money for anything they want from the shop.

I sure am unhappy with the Reds over here on Uncle's land. They seem right uppity. They just don't do what they're told anymore. Think they're as good as us these days!

Let's hope they produce lots of nottocs this year, anyway. Lots of ginning for us, eh!

Your brother, Dave.

Landowner's accounts for Year 10

Table rent	Amount owed	Ginning fees	No. of gins 5 rollads per gin	Amount owed
Tenant 1	30 rollads	Tenant 1	6	30 rollads
Tenant 2	30 rollads	Tenant 2	5	25 rollads
Tenant 3	30 rollads	Tenant 3	6	30 rollads
Tenant 4	30 rollads	Tenant 4	6	30 rollads
		Smallholder	10	50 rollads

Money borrowed for shop supplies	Amount borrowed	Interest at 20%	Total
Tenant 1	20 rollads	4 rollads	24 rollads
Tenant 2	20 rollads	4 rollads	24 rollads
Tenant 3	20 rollads	4 rollads	24 rollads
Tenant 4	20 rollads	4 rollads	24 rollads
Smallholder	0 rollads	0 rollads	0 rollads

	Owed from last year	Owed from this year	Total debt	Payments from tenants	Still owed next year
Tenant 1	30 rollads	84 rollads	114 rollads	50 rollads	64 rollads
Tenant 2	25 rollads	79 rollads	104 rollads	45 rollads	59 rollads
Tenant 3	30 rollads	84 rollads	114 rollads	50 rollads	64 rollads
Tenant 4	20 rollads	84 rollads	104 rollads	50 rollads	54 rollads
Smallholder	0 rollads	50 rollads	50 rollads	50 rollads	0 rollads

(Don't forget to pay the shop for what the tenants have had at the end of the year)

To give a starting point, Year 11 (Round 1) has the cost of ginnings and interest rates set, as are debts owed carried over from the previous year. Forms for subsequent years are blank, since rates are set by the landowner and debts created in the action.

Landowner's accounts for Year 11 (12, 13, etc.)

Table rent	Amount owed	Ginning fees	No. of gins 5 r per gin	Amount owed
Tenant 1	............rollads	Tenant 1	....	............rollads
Tenant 2	............rollads	Tenant 2	....	............rollads
Tenant 3	............rollads	Tenant 3	....	............rollads
Tenant 4	............rollads	Tenant 4	....	............rollads
		Smallholder	....	............rollads

Money borrowed for shop supplies	Amount borrowed	Interest at 20%	Total
Tenant 1	............rollads	............rollads	............rollads
Tenant 2	............rollads	............rollads	............rollads
Tenant 3	............rollads	............rollads	............rollads
Tenant 4	............rollads	............rollads	............rollads
Smallholder	............rollads	............rollads	............rollads

	Owed from last year	Owed from this year	Total debt	Payments from tenants	Still owed next year
Tenant 1	64 rollads	....	....	....	....
Tenant 2	59 rollads	....	....	....	....
Tenant 3	64 rollads	....	....	....	....
Tenant 4	54 rollads	....	....	....	....
Smallholder	0 rollads	....	....	....	....

(Don't forget to pay the shop for what the tenants have had at the end of the year)

DESIGNING A SIMULATION: *ROLL OF THUNDER* 59

At the end of the year . . .

Fill in your accounts sheet for that year.

Tell your tenants in writing what they owe you and whether this is for ginning, table rent or borrowing money to buy from the shop. What they can't pay will go onto your accounts sheet for the next year.

Decide how much interest you will charge for borrowing money the next year.

Decide how much rent you will charge next year.

Make any other decisions you think are necessary.

THE YELLOW SHOPKEEPER

Running the shop

You buy your supplies from the wholesaler (you may see him also buying nottocs from the tenants).

These supplies are scissors, paper and coloured pencils.

You sell these supplies on to the tenants on the estate and to the family who own the smallholding. You can charge what you want.

If you charge too much they may not buy. If they don't buy you go bust!

When you sell an item keep a record of the item, how much it was sold for and who it was sold to. You have an accounts sheet for this purpose. If your customer couldn't pay cash, then at the end of the year you can show your accounts to the landowner who will give you the money the customers owe you. They will owe the landowner who may charge them interest for the loan.

Negotiate with the landowner how much in debt your customers can be. If they borrow a million rollads, they will never pay that back!

This is how to keep your accounts sheet.

Shopkeeper's accounts

Customer	Item sold	Amount	Cash or credit?
Tenant 12	paper (2 sheets)	10 rollads	credit

At the end of the year you would ask the landowner for the 10 rollads. Tenant 12 would then owe the landowner.

The Yellow shopkeeper does not get a completed accounts sheet like the landowners, tenants and smallholders, since the shop would have had debts paid by the landowner and wiped the slate clean at the end of the last year.

Shopkeeper's accounts for Year 11 (12, 13, etc.)

Customer	Item sold	Amount	Cash or credit?
....	....	....	....
....	....	....	....
....	....	....	....
....	....	....	....

At the end of the year . . .

Inform the landowner of how much he or she owes you for things the tenants and smallholders bought (if they couldn't pay cash). You should have kept a record on your accounts sheet.

Inform the smallholders and tenants in writing of how much they bought. Show them if they paid cash or if they owe the landowner.

Make any decisions for next year.

THE RED SHOPKEEPER

The Red shopkeeper comes into operation a year later (Year 12) than the Yellow shopkeeper and thus this document which they receive at the start of the simulation.

Read this first!!!

Year 10 is nearly over and Year 11 is about to begin.

You are a Red. You plan to set up a shop supplying nottoc makers in a year's time. First you want to work for a year with a Red family to see the customer's side of things. You are going to live with a tenant family on the Yellow estate (see their map) for Year 11. You will start to run your shop several miles away in Year 12.

Other documents are the same as the Yellow shopkeeper with the exception that all references to the landowner are changed to the wholesaler. These documents are given to the Red shopkeeper at the start of Year 12.

Each role set receives this map at the start of the simulation (the Red shop does not come into existence until Round 2 (Year 12)):

Yellow estate

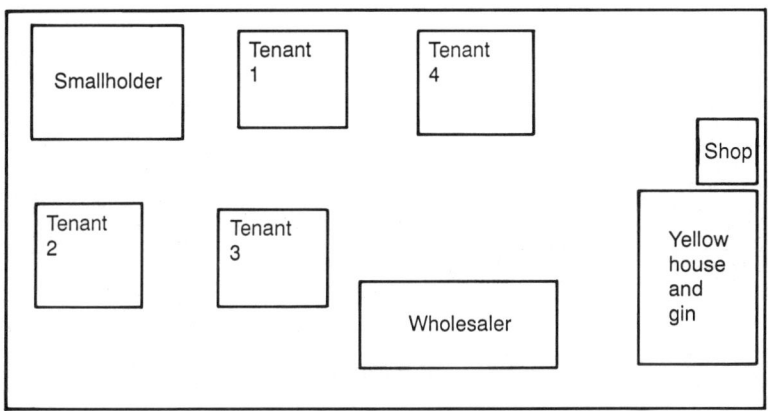

Role badges are included with the documents for Round 1.

CONTROLLER

These are the Controller's notes I used on the day the simulation was run. They are idiosyncratic and would need to be developed significantly if they were to be used by anyone other than the author. They are brief and cover the fundamentals. They give an indication of the kinds of areas to be included. The map is included in the notes to save looking through the other simulation documents.

Controller's notes

Setting up
Sort classroom according to map

Yellow Estate

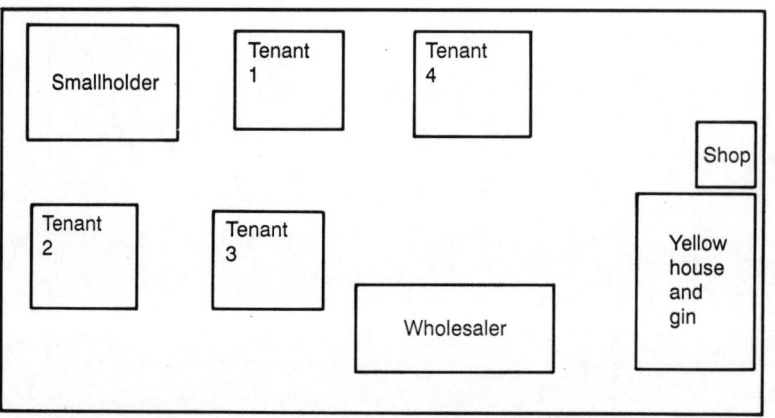

Role allocation

Mathematician in each group.
Strong people for Yellow roles – 2 landowners and 2 shopkeepers.
Other role allocation as negotiated with teacher.

2 Yellow landowners
2 Yellow shopkeepers
2 Red shopkeepers
4 tenants in each of three groups
4 smallholders
(absences from tenants)

Instructions
School bags to the front.

Controller's notes

Give out resources

Document packs for Round 1: 'Papers not in any order', 'Wear badges'.

Tenants – 1 pair of poor scissors, 4 sheets of paper, 2 different coloured pencils each, nottoc stencil, 5 rollads.

Smallholder – 2 pairs of good scissors, 6 sheets of paper, 3 different coloured pencils, nottoc stencil, 50 rollads.

Landowner – ginner, 1000 rollads.

Yellow shopkeeper – 100 rollads.

Wholesaler/buyer – spare resources, i.e. pencils, paper, scissors, stencils, 5000 rollads.

Briefing

State that it is the end of Year 10. Simulation lasts 3 rounds until end of Year 13 (may be less). During year you work. End of year you do accounts and make decisions. Look through your documents and work out who you are and what you have to do. Remember this is the end of Year 10. Some of your information may not apply until a later time.

Start Year 11

Buyer
Ginned nottocs worth about 10 rollads each (adjust as necessary and according to market).

Wholesaler
Sell only to shop!

Paper – 3 rollads each sheet
Scissors – 100 rollads each
Pencils – 50 rollads each

End Year 11 when smallholders produce about 9 ginned nottocs.

'Complete "At the end of the year" tasks'.

> **Controller's notes**
>
> Give documents to new shopkeeper and money – 100 rollads.
>
> **Start Year 12**
>
> **End Year 12** (as 11).
>
> **Start Year 13**
>
> **End Year 13** (as 11 and 12)
>
> **Debrief**

The simulation did not follow the Controller's notes – the debrief took place at the end of Year 12 and then a further round was run. There is discussion of this in 'Running the simulation'.

Fine-tuning

As I mentioned in the last chapter, simulations will always need testing and on-going refinement. There are many ways in which I would improve on the initial design of *Roll of Thunder* as I have described it here, but there were two areas in particular which were seriously miscalculated and which are quite likely to cause problems in the design of other systems simulations.

The first was to do with the mathematical relationships. I had set the market price for the nottocs incorrectly (the controller bought the finished nottocs from the tenants and smallholders) so that the poverty trap for the tenants' counterparts in the book was not properly reflected. It's a bit difficult to explain without seeing the model in operation, but it's like players in *Monopoly* collecting £1 000 000, rather than the usual £200, every time they pass 'Go' while maintaining other values as they usually are – for example, keeping the estate value of a station at £200. I had to amend this during the run by getting a feel for what was happening. This would normally lead to more detailed analysis afterwards.

In relation to this, timing affected the whole mathematical equation. The less a tenant produced in a round the more severe the loss, because the rent did not change – it was still 30 rollads in the first round whether the tenant produced one or twenty nottocs. The nottocs were taking much longer to produce than I expected, as explained in the last chapter, and I had to accept a lower output per round to avoid each round lasting for a boring eternity. I had thus to make adjustments to the system to take account of this.

The accounts generally need further tidying up. For example, it was only after running the simulation that I realized that the landowner's accounts sheets only charge interest on credit given for purchases at the shop rather than on all the credit (for example, for ginning and rent) that was given where tenants couldn't pay. This minimized the difference in terms of the debt trap between those in debt and those who weren't, although this was still effective.

The second problem was to do with another outcome of the problem of timing I have mentioned. Since it took far longer than I had anticipated for tenants and smallholders to produce nottocs, this left the landowners with very little to do for much of the time. I adjusted this during the run by accepting a reduction in the quality of the nottocs which I explained was acceptable because of 'a shortage in the market'. Production was still low but the situation was slightly improved.

The simulation might be fine-tuned to reflect some finer distinctions between the sharecroppers and the smallholders as they are described in the book. For example, in the book (Taylor 1990: 77) it is suggested that the sharecroppers do not sell their cotton (as the tenants do in the simulation) but receive a percentage after the cotton is sold by the landowner. This kind of detail might be useful information for the participants, but has little impact on the fundamental principles of the system and simulation objectives.

Reflections

Despite the limitations of the model relating to the social dimension of the system which I discussed earlier, the simulation was fruitful as a comparative means of exploring the text as the discussion of the debrief in Chapter 5 shows. I did have some concerns despite this success both at the time of writing the simulation and retrospectively, which are shared below.

The half-hearted attempt at representing the social environment through the letters to participants failed abysmally, particularly because I could not represent the long-term nature of indoctrination in the real world. The shopkeepers and landowners quickly forgot the letters (as they were to say in the debrief) and just got on with the business side of things.

I had a problem with indoctrinating the yellow (white) community. Could I actually encourage racist attitudes, even though I was using metaphors for black and white (red and yellow) in the simulation? Perhaps I am overrating the power of the simulation in asking this question, but this needs careful consideration. I think this is why I shied away from more substantial indoctrination in a first round. I had planned quite deep indoctrination of the yellow (white) community using mythology about the slave status of the red (black) participants. The blacks (reds) would have been made aware of their own history of oppression and violation. From here the social attitudes might have worked quite well in informing the economic system. Not going ahead in this way was probably cowardice on my part. Instead, they had the rather tokenistic letters from relatives.

There is a risk with systems simulations of oversimplification. I felt this was very much the case with *Roll of Thunder*. There is a danger that participants will have gone away with a view that all the white people in the text (in general?) are racist oppressors and indeed that the issue is no more complex than black and white (no pun intended). There were two people in the text who were significant in demonstrating that not all white people were racist. The first of these was a young boy who risked ridicule from other whites and probably vociferous action from his racist parents, to befriend the brother of the black central character, Cassie. He was significant for defying the expectations of the white community by turning up in support at times when the wrath of the white community was most visible. As I mentioned earlier, a white lawyer supports the boycott by backing the mortgages and credit of the black people, and he helps to save the life of a black boy from a vigilante mob at the end of the novel. Such complexities might conveniently be left out for the sake of simple operation of the model, and indeed I could not find a way to include this dimension in the causal network of economic blackmail which underpinned the simulation. Such issues need to be unpicked during the debrief, though one can't help wondering if the behaviour of the simulation won't be more powerful and lasting than the discussion that followed.

There is a danger, as with any simulation that tries to explore an existing reality, of confusion in the minds of participants as to what was the 'reality' of the book and what was the fiction of the simulation. An example of this might be the hostile relationship which developed between the smallholders and the tenants (discussed further in Chapter 5), which was quite different to the supportive relationship described by Mildred D. Taylor.

Further ideas

1 The simulation could have been followed by a public meeting to discuss the situation. The meeting might have been called by the tenants, or by the landowners prompted by a black boycott of white resources. It is conceivable that the participants, having worked within the system, could have set their own agenda, deciding the issues that need following up.
2 The author has died before completion of *Roll of Thunder, Hear My Cry*. What are the likely processes which follow this? A meeting of publisher, in-house writers . . .? How will the work be completed? What style? Certain draft areas of the text need reworking. How could language exploration be built into this? This could be a long-term simulation, structured by the professional environment of a publishing house, which could frame a few weeks' work, or a shorter simulation using only small sections of the text.

3 I could have taken an incident from the text and built a simulation around this. For example, in *Roll of Thunder, Hear My Cry*, Cassie is pushed off the sidewalk by a white girl. Her racist father supports her to Cassie's horror. Any number of simulations could have been developed from this. For example, if one wanted to question this in terms of contemporary social values, one could set up a social services case conference documented by current legislation and procedures. Behaviour, events and circumstances in the text could have been brought to bear as documentation on the committee's proceedings.

4 Running the simulation

All kinds of subtexts operate during the running of a simulation which will affect the extent and nature of the 'reality' experienced by participants as a social, emotional and intellectual event. A simulation is never simply defined by the planned objectives and structures of the author; each run is different, and although the simulation may appear to be more or less the same from the outside, the internal reality will vary for the individual participant according to the specific circumstances surrounding her on each occasion. The role of the controller is critical to the experiences which will take place.

Setting up the simulation

If possible, run through the simulation if you are unfamiliar with it, with a small group of colleagues or friends. If this is impossible, try to run through it yourself from various of the role perspectives. This will allow you to deliver your role as controller more smoothly, including knowing when to input new information/ resources, and when to set up changes in the scenario or new rounds. Try to visualize who might say or do what and what kind of interaction is likely to take place. Things may not turn out as you visualize them, but you will have a better grasp of what is going on.

You may need to arrange to have the timetable changed to allow enough time for the simulation to take place. This was the case when I ran the *Roll of Thunder* simulation. Simulations are usually meaningless if they are 'cut up' into a number of forty-minute slots, particularly when they are communications simulations (unless they are designed to be that short). The whole point of simulations is that they establish meaningful functional roles which are heavily invested in and I can only refer the reader to Chapter 6 and ask whether Ami could possibly have achieved that intensity of involvement and emotion if she had sporadically gone off to other lessons. Some teachers may find this unavoidable if the use of a simulation is not deemed important enough to outweigh the sometimes real inconvenience of timetable manipulation. You may also need to sort out another classroom, if your role sets represent different communities for example. This is where your kind words to the teacher in the next classroom over the last two weeks pays off.

Make sure you have all the documentation you need. Do you have enough materials for the numbers who will attend? Check all equipment carefully *immediately* before the simulation. Have the tape-recorders got batteries in? Are the clocks in different rooms synchronized if they need to be? Is the computer program, which forms an essential part of the simulation, still on the disk which you neatly labelled 'simulation disk' the year before, or has it been wiped? Be particularly careful where information technology is involved and give the materials a run through if possible.

The reality of certain kinds of simulation can be enhanced by simple environmental features – maybe a map on a wall, or other simple clues to the 'other' reality (than the classroom). This gives participants something to latch onto and is particularly useful early on when the momentum is slow.

In language/communications simulations, the social/communicative/ linguistic experience can be profoundly affected by the physical organization of the environment. I ran a simulation, based on the Treaty of Versailles, on different occasions to quite different effect because of the different arrangement of furniture on each occasion. In the simulation, nations from opposing sides in the First World War consider where responsibility for the War should lie. If one long table was used, with the Allies on one side and the Alliance on the other, the nature of the interaction was confrontational, hostile, with sharp intonation prompting one year this comment from a member of the British contingent: 'We won the World Cup in 1966 anyway!' There was some intrusion into the reality of the simulation here – but that's not the point. The same simulation run with the parties *around* a table – much like the organization of the United Nations – produced different social attitudes and language based on compromise, negotiation and courtesy.

If you don't want different groups to share information with each other in a simulation, you will have to construct this by providing appropriate space. I have seen simulations where secrecy has been intended by the simulation authors and the controller has had to step in to require this where students were leaning over their chairs and comparing notes because of their close proximity. Simulation instructions usually, but not always, describe physical arrangements. These always need consideration by the teacher or controller.

The reality of the simulation can be helped by having everything in place before the students enter the room. This saves you fussing around for ten minutes, giving things out, and it will arouse the curiosity of the students. You will have done a lot of the work in setting the agenda in this way.

It may be desirable before the briefing or before the action to ask students to leave their bags or equipment in a place away from where the action will take place, if such equipment is to be supplied in organized and limited quantities as part of the simulation. If the participants will require scissors for example, and a key power relationship is that one group starts off with more scissors than another, this relationship might be upset if someone turns out a bag of scissors during the action.

The briefing

Although it is not always possible, since this is often dependent on the author's materials, I prefer to introduce the simulation from the 'inside' (intrinsically). Any text or instructions can be delivered to the students when they are already in role. So, for example, the roles or the issue at the heart of a simulation could be delivered through a tour brochure or an issue-based pamphlet (see Chapter 2). I introduced key information for the simulation in Chapter 6 in this way. The functional roles of the participants were given in a meeting by me in role as the vicar at the church hall:

> Welcome to our church hall once again. A television crew from TV South West are visiting us next week. They want to know something about our community – the interests we have and so on . . .

This is the first information they had on the simulation.

> Now Mr Terry . . . perhaps if your sports club could give us a bit of a talk . . .

and so the roles were allotted and the immediate task (this one was not the central issue of the simulation) made clear in the context of the simulation world. The fabric of the community and the simulation was gradually being built up around the students (or the members of the community).

This is important because in the simulation participants need key information and they need to refer back to instructions and other information to function consistently in their roles. To reiterate the point in Chapter 2, the reality of the simulation is more likely to be maintained if they refer back to an internal register rather than the register of a pre-simulation situation of teacher/facilitator giving instructions to students, the external reality which one is trying to suspend.

If the author's documents are extrinsic (i.e. they talk to the student),

> You are Inspector Smith

rather than intrinsic (i.e. they talk to the role),

> Dear Inspector Smith

there is no reason why you can't convert them, usually quite easily, to intrinsic documents.

This approach can help to construct a reality, but it can also make life difficult for some students who may find it hard to latch on to the environment which is being gradually built up around them. It can be much easier to simply describe the environment for them by, for example, giving out documents which simply say 'You are Inspector Smith and you have to do this, this and this'. This will not demand much imagination of the teacher or student and this itself is perhaps an area of learning lost. Usually, some intrinsic mechanism can be found to make it clear who is who and what their function is. Prior viewing of a 'television documentary' about the case in which Inspector Smith and her team are involved might clarify the roles, situation and task. It is, though, important not to pre-empt the character of Inspector Smith or other roles in the simulation, but only to identify the circumstances in which the roles operate.

Avoid phrases like 'Play (or take) your roles seriously', which are so tempting, to make the simulation go well. If the participants don't take their roles seriously, then there is something wrong with the simulation. By doing this one enters the realm of acting – of extrinsic controls and extrinsic awareness by the participants as I have explained. These kinds of comments are likely to occur if you are briefing as teacher rather than as controller from within the simulation as I have described.

Equally, comments like 'Do not give the game away', where some role sets have secret information or objectives, 'You want to win the case' or 'Give only some information away' (these are actual briefing quotes) are unacceptable from the controller during the briefing, since they represent interference to the point that the activity is no longer a simulation. The *participants* should decide whether or not to give secrets away. Don't compensate for bad design, or ruin a good one, in the briefing – change the simulation or stay out! Any of the above comments might be acceptable from a controller in role, but even then such advice must reflect what one would expect from that role in the real situation. Your boss might tell you what your objectives are, for example, but this is not the same as when such guidance is given in the briefing, since anything said in the action may be rejected.

All participants need to have *meaningful* roles. Where there are not enough roles to go round, more than one participant can take a role. It is important to maintain reality here as elsewhere. Two people with one voice may keep the planned balance of roles, but if two people are 'Inspector Smith' much realism is lost. Each participant could have separate identities, for example Inspector Smith and her sergeant, but work as a team, negotiating their final agreed input into information sharing points in the simulation structure.

It would be very unwise to exclude any of the simulation roles if the numbers in the group don't match up with those available unless you know exactly what you are doing. Every role presumably will have a function in the simulation and it could fail if any of these are removed. Of course, if there are eight 'conservationists' or 'residents' or 'jurists' and there is no discernible distinction between them, it is likely that you won't cause any problems if you take one out.

Do you pick certain students for particular roles? Selecting roles in this way can be appropriate, but this depends on what you want. It may be that certain students in a class will not work well together however acclaimed a simulation might be, and so you may choose for them not to be in close proximity. It may be that some members will be more suited to certain roles than others. If you choose a good speaker, for example, to take a role which seems to demand this, you may be setting up an exciting or workable simulation, but at the same time depriving other people of the learning experience of speaking by not selecting them if they're deemed weak here. In any case, it is always difficult to predict how students will behave in a simulation. Chapter 6 describes the dramatically uncharacteristic (in usual classroom terms) responses of two students in a simulation.

It is important to disassemble the usual power structures of the class. In particular, if a teacher is involved in the simulation as controller, any power relationship (usually of teacher authority) should be disassembled. For many teachers, this may mean moving from imperative language ('Move if you can't see!') to a more negotiating style. In introducing simulations where I still have the function of teacher/facilitator, I try to transfer authority through a greater emphasis on this negotiating style: 'Can you see alright?', 'Would you like to move?'

Give participants, where possible within the materials, the opportunity to ask questions. Simulations can be complex, and participants have to understand how they relate to each other, what their main and other objectives are, what resources they can use, and how, and so on. In an extrinsic briefing, where the teacher introduces the simulation as teacher before the action starts, this can take the simple form of questions and answers. In an intrinsic briefing, devices will need to be implemented. For example, a government minister may set up a task for a commission through a briefing which allows questions and answers. Ultimately, though, this is a question of design, and documents in the simulation should allow all participants to function fully. Don't invent roles for this purpose which will conflict with or detract from the original structures.

Documents provided by the simulation author may require adaptation for all or some of the students in a class. It is important, however the briefing is carried out, to be sure that all the documents are understood, or that there is opportunity for them to be understood. This might mean consideration of role allocation before the simulation and preparing documents for students with particular roles. It might mean ensuring there is group support available during the simulation.

During the action

You will need to be aware of what participants should be doing at any given point in the simulation if this is in someway planned in the design. I included in the design of the *Roll of Thunder* simulation a grid (shown in Chapter 3, p. 48) which showed who would be doing what with whom and with what during each round. If this kind of mapping is not provided in a simulation you are using, it is well worth producing one yourself. This is particularly useful, I have found, as a reminder of when I, as controller, have had to give out resources, but also in case participants lose their way for some reason.

Simulations are slow to get started. It takes a while for participants to understand their roles, purpose, relationships and the other information around them. It takes a while for motivation to take hold. Don't panic and start urging people on.

Don't offer help where you wouldn't in the real-life situation. Be there as banker or computer technician only. Don't engage in aside conversations about homework. The best way to deal with people who ask for your help as teacher is, in role, not to understand. Be careful, though. You can hurt some students' feelings by appearing to ignore them. Where participant behaviour does disrupt the activity, say in the case of an argument relating to issues outside of the simulation, one can diffuse this with more effect in role than as teacher. Try to diffuse the situation without causing disruption to the other participants.

Most of all don't *hover*. Teachers often feel they ought to be doing more. They can feel guilty about their lack of participation. Hovering makes participants self-conscious, especially at the start when their own identities and sense of purpose are weak. This is just the time when your own identity is unestablished and you need to feel useful. Again, would you hover in the actual situation? If you need to be present (you will in the classroom), make your presence purposeful either by being in role, preferably, or by appearing detached from the participant activity.

You will probably be making notes about your observations of the action. Try to do this unobtrusively if you don't have a role, or you will again make the participants self-conscious. One of the critical aspects of the action noted by Tansey and Unwin (1969: 6) in their observation of a simulation was that the '... freedom from censure permitted and even encouraged adventurous play'. If you have an intrinsic role, you will probably be able to disguise your note-taking fairly easily.

Where you feel things are going wrong, or not the way you would like, but the participants are acting within the frame of the simulation, don't be tempted to interfere. In one simulation I have seen, different groups were decoding secret documents. The designer had intended the groups to be in competition. One participant in the room could break the codes rather well and he promptly displayed his knowledge by helping to decode documents for all the other groups. The controller quickly interjected that they were not supposed to be helping each other. For him, this was not the way to do things. But maybe the participant wasn't or didn't want to be competitive. If there was a culture of secrecy, established through the history of the organization (shown in intrinsic documents) or the physical separation of the groups and this impacted on the participants, then fine. But this shouldn't be left to the controller. The time for the controller to inject views on the simulation is in the debrief. If some groups were supposed to struggle with the codes, then this might be raised here.

Where there is clearly destructive behaviour it will be obvious.

Try to avoid caricature where the controller has a role – this will quickly spiral into caricature behaviour by participants. If the controller declares in the briefing, 'This is where I do my Inspector Morse impersonation', this will create a comical atmosphere closer to *Spitting Image* than a murder inquiry. The controller has a lot of power and every signal carries a lot of weight in terms of permission regarding behaviour. It is best to allow the participants to define their own behaviour.

5 The debrief

The debrief is the most critical stage of the simulation process. It is an opportunity to externalize students from their experience as participants and to allow them to reflect on their behaviour and the course of events in the simulation. Their view, in the debrief, of that behaviour and the system and relationships which operated around them in the simulation is likely to be very different from their view as participants.

The debrief also identifies the focus or objectives of the simulation. Submerged in the action, the simulation could be about any number of things to a participant, and probably different things to different participants with their discrete views of the whole. A simulation intended by the designer or controller to be about conservation or the world of finance might well seem to be of more significance to some as a simulation about power and language. Simulations, even where they are 'models of reality' taking a specific unitary segment of that reality, are by nature still interdisciplinary events.

Even where the simulation is designed primarily for the development of performative skills through participation in the action of the simulation – for language experience, for example – it is essential to have a debrief to avoid a sense of anti-climax at the sudden conclusion of a dynamic reality (the action) which is at least going to leave questions like 'Why?' and 'What was going on?' looming large in the minds of students as they leave the room at the end of any simulation. After running the simulation discussed in Chapter 6, I had very little time for a debrief (a significant failure). I had children accosting me in the corridors as I was leaving the school still arguing excitedly about the issue. In this case, the debrief is as vital for emotional reasons as for intellectual ones. In any case, it is a wasted opportunity if the experience of the simulation is not deconstructed in the debrief and in a sense without a debrief there is no point to a simulation since one cannot examine the reality, whether it be of communication or an economic system, in the light of the simulated experience.

If the simulation was successful, the participants will want to share their excitement and their experiences. It is important to allow this to happen so that they can 'come down' as I have described. However, it is important to derole or rerole students so that they can look objectively (*externally* might be better) at their experiences and it could be problematic if the language of the debrief is socially constructed as it was in the simulation , i.e. 'You were horrible – I'll get you for that'. 'You were horrible' is fine, but this now has to be framed in the detached language and perspective of the debrief rather than the participant language, behaviour and attitudes of the simulation. They have to shift their thinking from a narrow to a broad view. Questions to particular groups or individuals about their experiences will introduce a more formal structure, at the same time allowing them to share and prevent this kind of emotive participant interaction.

Participants might be allowed to enjoy a 'chaotic' spell before such questioning to get things out of their system. It can be important to consolidate feelings and attitudes which may not have been given explicit expression in the simulation, before then deconstructing them. This can be a useful 'transitional' phase. In the debrief of the *Roll of Thunder* simulation (discussed at the end of this chapter), I allowed two role sets – tenants and smallholders – to express a hostility at the start of the debrief, although this had not been planned. During the simulation, they had been working in an antithetical relationship but they had not been able to express their view or feelings about this to each other. When the action ended, they threw accusations at each other about their respective attitudes in the action: 'You lot were selfish!', 'Well you should have worked harder!' The expression of this hostility, having been made explicit, could then be evaluated in terms of the system as a whole which had led to this relationship. This was also useful in generating part of the debriefing agenda from what the participants considered to be important.

It is vital that all parts of the simulation – the essential documentation, roles, functions, problems and powers – are shared to give an overview in which analysis can take place. Each role set should be asked to explain how they fitted into the system, how they responded and what the motives were for their actions. If the debrief is to take snapshots of the action at different stages, the teacher might ask each role set to share this information as discussion of each stage of the action arises. The first questions should be straightforward and might be along the lines of:

What did you think the simulation was about?
What was your role in it?
What problems did you have to solve?
How did you do this?

You may have decided on a very structured debrief involving principles which must be examined in a certain way. Very often the kinds of questions given above will lead to complex analyses despite their straightforward nature.

The debrief could be carried out in role. At the end of a manufacturing simulation, there could be a meeting to discuss the annual report with a given brief from the General Manager (who is on holiday) on aspects of the running of the company to be covered. The participants should shift from their original roles, and rerole say from factory workers and managers to an outside consultancy. If the participants don't rerole, this may lead to the kind of short-sightedness and an inability to decentre which I described above.

It is vital that the students stay in touch with the feelings and experiences they had in the simulation as this is an important basis for analysis in the debrief and I would therefore recommend that the debrief, or at least an initial debrief, is not postponed beyond a break time. Jones (1987: 88–9) does suggest that there are advantages to delaying the debrief for longer periods, particularly because participants will be able to offer 'mature reflection' and the controller will be able to think through what she saw. In this case, it might be advisable to use video so that the students can stay in touch with their experiences. Feelings and meanings experienced in the simulation inform discussion and much intuitive understanding could be lost with time.

Debriefing questions are likely to be provided in a simulation by the designer which will relate to the educational purposes of the simulation. It is likely, however, since every simulation will take a different course, that the controller will be able to formulate questions based on her observations of the specific experiences/behaviour in each run of the simulation. The controller is likely to be the only person in the room who can offer an external perspective on things (or at least a controller's perspective), although as each group shares ideas from its perspective this will offer in a jigsaw fashion an externalized, or broader, 'reality'. Thus observations made during the simulation will be as important as those which are defined at the design or planning stage.

This is not to suggest that the debrief should be entirely controlled by the controller – there should be an opportunity for the participants to take over some of the debriefing agenda. The participants are likely to have questions to ask and insights to offer which may not occur to the controller. Nor can the controller be held to be 'right' or provide right answers any more at this stage than in the simulation itself. The participants may have been operating very subtle techniques, not visible to the controller, which may have been seen from the outside as too passive without a full understanding of the social, emotional and other pressures operating in the simulation. It is also worth bearing in mind that it can be injurious to challenge the participants' feelings and conclusions directly and they would be quite justified in asking 'How would you know?' The controller is as likely to raise issues, areas of discussion and to ask questions as she is to explain what happened.

Some simulations include questionnaires which participants fill in at the start of the debrief. This can be quite useful in protecting the students where criticism of their actions in the simulation might take place. It also provides a structure for response where questioning might be intimidating and more difficult to respond to. Questionnaires can also, however, dictate the content of the debrief to the point that the agenda is decided substantially or entirely by the questionnaire format.

It can be useful to allow the students to stay with their role sets during the debrief even though they have de- or reroled. This might take place in the form of small group work. They can then share their experiences, exploring commonalities and differences in a secure environment. On the other hand, another useful strategy is to mix role sets, again in small groups, so that they can gasp in amazement at the perspective of their 'opponents' (perhaps) which they didn't grasp during the action. Despite the sharing of information in whole group debriefs the 'other side' can still be remote and their views not really accepted or understood.

A debrief does not have to be the final stage of a simulation. One might use a debrief as the basis for a further round or a rerun of a simulation. This could test any hypotheses formed. In the *Roll of Thunder* simulation, the participants thought that during the debrief they had established the mechanisms for power within the simulation and the means to alter the system from the way it had operated in the first couple of rounds. I hadn't planned a further run but decided to see how the participants would apply their new-found knowledge and understanding. In fact, their behaviour changed in some ways and a further debrief (see p. 81) was able to explore this. Their view of the system in the second debrief was quite different from their view in the first. They had developed a more deterministic view of the system which they had begun to see as irresistible.

Where a simulation is based on a 'model of reality', it is important to explore thoroughly the experience of the participants before turning to discussion of the situation being simulated. Early references to the reality will externalize participants' thinking and this may define or inhibit their feelings and ideas. It is better to consolidate the experience of the simulation so that the participants can connect in a meaningful way with the actual system.

The participants will have exposed themselves in all kinds of ways in the action of the simulation – their behaviour in the action may have been selfish, hostile, arrogant – all the things they would not wish to identify themselves with in their everyday lives. Students should *never* feel threatened as a result of this in the debrief. It is important to distance the student from the role and to protect her from personal attack (by her 'victims' in the action, for example) in relation to this. It is also worth bearing in mind that students should not be made to feel they have failed because they did not behave in the way the debrief suggests they might, would or should have in real life. Reducing this kind of sensitivity is one reason why it is important to derole or rerole.

Debriefing *Roll of Thunder*

What follows is the debrief of *Roll of Thunder*, the context and design of which are discussed in Chapter 3. This section aims really to consolidate Chapter 3, since the outcomes described here tie in with some of the design objectives in that chapter, and to suggest the kinds of learning which might occur in a debrief.

The early questions in the debrief were not tied to the text. I wanted the participants to explore their own feelings and decisions first, to consolidate these and *then* to compare them.

PB:	How could the system be changed?
Red Tenant:	We think all the reds should get together and tell the landlords [owners] that they're charging us too much . . . then if they say no, then we can threaten to take our custom elsewhere . . . and if they threaten to chuck us off the land, then they won't get any income.
PB:	What do the landowners say to that?
Yellow Landowner:	There'd be more people wouldn't there!
PB:	So you'd just get someone else?

The debrief achieved quite a sophisticated understanding of the complex issues and relationships of power in the text (although at this stage we weren't discussing the text), based on the experience of both being oppressed by this system and operating this oppression. In response to my question about how the system might be changed, the oppressed identified the same mechanism as those in the text – the idea of group solidarity aimed at destruction of the oppressor's economy as can be seen in this and the following dialogue. They recognized not only the mechanism, or weapon, but the likely consequence:

Red Tenant:	. . . if they threaten to chuck us off the land, then they won't get any income

Equally the landowners recognized the extent of their power

There'd be more people wouldn't there!

And later on . . .

Red Tenant:	We're not using that table there . . . we can just say to them we're not going to pay the rent on that table there.
Yellow Landowner:	We could charge them the same on that one [the remaining table].
Red Tenant:	We're gonna say we'll pay this much [for the table]. That's what it's worth and if you don't like it . . .

Again they could see here the rent as a key blackmailing tool of the landowners as well as a means to respond to this. The rent starts to emerge as a key to the poverty trap, particularly as they recognize how the smallholders, a wealthier group, don't pay rent. This becomes the basis of a further means of action. As before, the landowners have a reply ready – they clearly understand the extent of their power!

Each role set was able to identify through the perspective of experience their perceived power in relation to others (here tenant to landowner and vice versa). Through the debrief, the two (here) perspectives then create something new – a more objective jigsaw of perspectives, with participants being brought to see what their roles may have blinded them to previously. The tenant threat in the first extract demonstrates that the landowner's power, shown in their reply 'There'd be more people wouldn't there!', was not available to the tenant's view initially.

This jigsaw continued to fit together and can be seen in the rather surprising response of the more successful smallholders in the next extract, who clearly had a very different view of the system:

> *(Indebted) Red Tenant:* If one group's in debt and another group's got a lot of money they can join together.
> *PB:* Would they do that? Would the wealthier people do that?
> *Same Red Tenant:* If they offered the people money for money [credit].
> *PB:* So you mean these nice people over here [the smallholders who did well in the simulation] could help you?
> *Red Smallholder:* [sarcastically] I don't think so!
> *Red Tenant:* When the debt's paid off they could pay some money back to the people that helped them.

This shows the start of a tension in the debrief between the tenants and the smallholders which continued to a later stage of the debrief:

> *PB:* Was this group of smallholders here, who are meant to be like the Logans, did they act like the Logans?
> *Red Tenant:* No . . . the Logans were willing to help their friends – but they didn't care.
> *Smallholder:* [aggressively] You never asked for any help!
> *PB:* [to tenants] Why do you think they [the smallholders] didn't help but the Logans did?
> *Red tenants:* They didn't really care about us but the Logans did.

The tenants were critical that smallholders didn't help them in the simulation.

The simulation smallholders were selfish during the action unlike in the text and quite unable, out of role, to empathize with the tenants during the early part of the debrief:

> *Red Smallholder:* They could buy their own land.
> *PB:* [to tenants] Why didn't you buy the land?
> *Red Tenant:* Didn't have enough money.
> *Red Smallholder:* We reckon they [the tenants] should work harder!
> *PB:* Because *you* worked hard?
> *Red Smallholder:* Yeah!
> *Red Tenant:* We were all working hard!
> *Red Tenant:* They had more money to start off with. They [the smallholders] were working the same rate as us and they were still getting more money.
> *Red Tenant:* We started off in debt – they didn't.

The smallholders were really pleased with themselves for having (as they saw it) achieved more – they thought they had earned it, since although they had more money than the others to start with they didn't need to use it. Their success actually depended on them having more and better resources from the outset and not having to pay rent.

This created a lot of discussion comparing the behaviour of the participants with that of the Logan family in the text. This then led on to why the Logans behaved differently in the book to those in the simulation? Were there different mechanisms for social behaviour in each? Different relationships? Why did the Logans act as generously as they did? Why, after all, should the smallholders have helped the rest?

It then came to light that the sharecroppers and smallholders identified with each other as black people in the text, whereas in the simulation the relationship between tenants and smallholders had been one of purely economic rivalry. Discussion of the common racial oppression which united the Logans with the sharecroppers, came through here if not in the action. Even though this situational difference could be seen as a weakness in the simulation, the comparative structure was strong enough for useful analysis of the text and these contrasts could come through.

After the first debrief, I ran another round of the simulation to see what impact this might have.

PB:	How come everybody's better off this time?
Red Tenant 1:	There was more equipment.
Red Tenant 2:	Shop gave resources cheaper.
Yellow Shopkeeper 1:	We just thought that if they work faster we make more money for ourselves.
Yellow Landowner:	If they [the tenants and smallholders] work harder it's better for you.

This was something of an unexpected area of discussion for me and it led us into quite complex and obscure analyses which I wouldn't necessarily have expected from the group. They were able to argue or at least raise the question from this that the yellow community could be more generous in its provision of resources to the red community, thus being of mutual benefit economically. The more the reds produce the more the yellows earn from them in ginning fees and resources sold. Generosity and cooperation would thus be better for all. Why wasn't this the case in the book then? This led on to whether the whites, like Granger or the Wallaces who owned the store (see Chapter 3), were in fact wealthy enough in the first place to provide more resources even for their own benefit in this way. This then led to whether it would have been ideologically (in the book as opposed to the simulation where they did become more generous) acceptable to have been more generous. It could be pointed out that in the book the point is made that the only thing the poor whites had was thinking they were better than blacks (Taylor 1990: 98):

> Mr Simms hold on to that belief [that the blacks aren't as good as the whites] harder than some other folks because they have little else to hold on to. For him to believe that he is better than we are makes him think that he's important, simply because he's white. (Mama)

This kind of detail, which makes concrete, complex general values and relationships, would have been unlikely to have been unpicked – or raised – without the simulation experience.

Although this was a predominantly economic model for reasons I explained in Chapter 3 and something of a compromise in this sense, as I indicated there, it did bear comparison (or contrast) with the text in a fruitful way and was tied to the broader socio-cultural-psychological aspects of the system the participants saw to exist in the text. What was a simple model of economic cause and effect (with tokenistic tinkering with social attitudes) became a skeleton on which to hang the complexity of muscle and nervous system with all its social, political and psychological aspects. What was missing was as much cause for its discussion as what was there. The participants were able to say, 'It wasn't like that!', as much as they were able to identify with how they thought it was.

One sees not only intellectual perspective in the dialogue above but an emergent *attitude* in the language used which suggests a deeper understanding of the relationships. I have suggested elsewhere that participants should 'come down' and derole during the debrief. These conflicting and invested-in perspectives were in fact useful for most of this debrief.

The students were not only able to make intellectual judgements about the system but they were able in many cases to engage emotionally within it. For some the unfairness of ever increasing debt, despite a fair day's work, was an emotionally charged issue and I'm sure they came closer to identifying with sharecropper Avery in the text who I quoted in an earlier chapter: 'Anytime they thinks we steppin' outa our *place*, they feels like they gotta stop us' (Taylor 1990: 50). The participants reached quite serious levels of despair as each year passed and they undertook their accounts. The injustice and injury would be about as close as any readers' commonsense idea of how sharecropper Avery must have felt.

I think probably many participants experienced feelings which could not be equated with the text. There was this sense of injury and injustice that the smallholders were not supportive of the tenants, whereas it was not so for their counterparts in the book. Therefore I did not, in some respects, achieve one of my objectives, emotional empathy. This is not a serious problem though. Participants should be aware of this distinction, since it was explored in the debrief and on rereading they will have an experiential and emotional perspective from which to explore their ideas. Even if the feelings were somewhat contrary to the book, at least they have a starting point at an emotional and engaged level to revisit the book – something of a meaningful perspective from which to view the *actual* relationships. And since no reader has the same view of any text, such feeling might enhance or provide original insight.

The distortion of the smallholder-sharecropper relationship in the simulation does highlight the need for care in the debrief. The difference between smallholder and sharecropper was not the focus of the text as the difference between their counterparts seemed to be in the debrief of the simulation and there was not the same kind of tension between them – it was just a reason for different feelings about how to, and the ability to, respond to white oppression, rather than a hostility. Was it helpful or distorting? Some may go away with distorted perspectives and understanding – that the immensely significant events which surrounded them were the centrally important events of the book (or other system). It was thus essential that I did address this distinction in the debrief so that it was clear that we were talking about *contrasting* behaviour between the two texts.

These examples from the *Roll of Thunder* simulation show the complex levels at which analysis can been facilitated by the *experience* of the simulation. The participants were able to identify significant elements of the system and relationships between these. They were able to identify the elements of oppression and of resistance, and they were able to explore possibilities for manipulating power. Many of the responses might have been expected by the author at the design stage; others were quite unexpected and may never have seen the light of day but for the actual and unique placement of the participant within the dynamic of the simulation.

The debrief is not, of course, the sum of the learning that takes place in the simulation. Much is imbued or inculturated, perhaps never to reach explicit recognition as learning, or it may be made consciously meaningful in a later context, perhaps in rereading the book.

6 The language experience

Taking part

Limiting functionality

Ami and Toni have just taken part in a communications simulation of the kind which opened the first chapter. The simulation is based on the issue of a building development near a community. Ami and Toni participated as residents. They have been completely unprimed. The following is an extract from a debrief with them:

PB: I asked people if they spoke in ways they don't normally speak. Are there things that happened this morning that don't normally happen in a lesson? Things that you learned or that you did?

Ami: I don't normally answer questions . . . I think I just took it too seriously.

PB: You took it *too* seriously?

Ami: Erm . . . I just got carried away.

PB: Was it too seriously or was it good that you took it seriously?

Ami: I had fun.

PB: 'Cos you are meant to take it seriously. You are meant to believe that you are the person you are.

Toni: I said more questions than . . . 'cos I wouldn't normally do that.

Ami: Yeah 'cos normally me and Toni just sit in the corner and never say anything.

Ami: In my report . . . it said in my old school that I . . . erm . . . don't talk when I've been asked a question.

Toni: Yeah and this way you get to express your feelings.

PB: So you actually *felt* things. What kind of things did you feel?

Ami: You feel angry because they want to spoil your village an' that . . . where you live.

PB: So is it because you were angry that you spoke?

Ami: I just . . . 'cos normally I don't speak 'cos I'm embarrassed . . . an' everyone's looking at me . . . um . . . but today I just ignored everyone – I just spoke.

PB: So you just . . . er . . . forget everything that was around you did you?
Toni: Yeah 'cos normally we get embarrassed 'cos everyone starts staring at you an' you get lost, but this time you ignore everyone around you.
Ami: I made it as if I was living in one of the houses an' it was gonna happen to me.
PB: Do you think . . . anyone else that you know . . . do you think they were acting differently to usual?
Ami: Yeah Michelle.
PB: How was she acting differently?
Ami: She's . . . I think she's normally a quiet one.
Toni: She really got angry.
Ami: She was really overreacting.

John Keen (1992: 4), in the context of discussing dialect, demonstrates the problems of communication between speakers of different dialects with a sample of students' comments about their experiences, including the following:

> . . . I couldn't say the things I wanted to say because . . . I though I'd say it wrong.
> (Sarah)

> . . . she use to say 'give up' instead of 'stop it' – we used to tease her about it.
> (Andrew)

The problem of communication is described by Keen as occurring '. . . more from nervousness internalised from social pressure than from absolute mutual unintelligibility' (ibid.: p. 4). People are afraid of getting it wrong, of not meeting social/linguistic expectation, or what Keen describes as the 'community norm' (p. 5). If I can lean on Keen a last time, for the moment, the task of learning to talk (or of learning to use language) is:

> . . . that a speaker . . . has to match language up with *social situations* and *roles*, to keep a *purpose* in mind, to compete with other speakers for a turn. The quality of speaking also depends on the nature of the *whole interaction* to which it contributes.
> (Keen 1992: 2, my emphases)

The classroom also offers up tremendous social pressures and expectations of the kind Keen is referring to above which seem to demand a conformity of speech, and which, as Ami and Toni's comments suggest, allow participation according to established socio-linguistic status. A rut of expectation develops about how you behave and how others will expect you to behave. Ami and Toni have a clear perception of this at a fairly generalized level in their description of Michelle: 'she's normally a quiet one'. And they certainly have a clear idea of their own socio-linguistic status in the group:

Ami: I don't *normally* answer questions . . .
Toni: I said more questions than . . . 'cos I wouldn't *normally* do that.
Ami: Yeah 'cos *normally* me and Toni just sit in the corner and never say anything.

Regular behavioural patterns build up among the members of a class which become fixed. Some students exude confidence, have a certain, consistent style to their language use, and even have a regular quantitative dominance of the language space. In fact, this was evident at the start of the simulation in which Toni and Ami took part; the regular class speakers dominated the oral space initially when roles were at an early stage of being defined and the usual classroom codes were still largely intact. In a sense, one might argue that Toni, Ami and their peers constructed their *own* functionality in the classroom – there are things they *normally* do and things they *normally* don't do. And it is in no way *only* the likes of Ami and Toni who are deprived of language experience in the school environment. Those who they might identify as outgoing and confident, exercising power through language, are themselves the victims of social, behavioural and linguistic conformity. The school pupils are all restricted in their linguistic behaviour by the limited number of social contexts in which they find themselves. There is a variety for the playground and a different variety for the interview with the teacher; a register for each of the social contexts of the school.

In explaining why this should be so in their case, Ami and Toni recognize the *social* and *emotional* basis for their non-participation, in the form of talk at least:

Ami: . . . normally I don't speak 'cos I'm embarrassed . . . an' everyone's looking at me.
Toni: Yeah 'cos normally we get embarrassed 'cos everyone starts staring at you an' you get lost . . .

Implicit in their comments about norms is that such fixed power relationships and ways of communicating are not normally challenged by their classroom activities. The classroom has created learned behavioural patterns which limit their language use.

Expanding functionality: New socio-linguistic environments

So what is it about the simulation which liberates Toni and Ami from the social norms and pressures of their classroom? The simulation provides both *diversity* of and *belief* in alternative socio-linguistic systems (to the usual classroom ones) – new social 'realities'. For Toni and Ami, the motivation for and character of their participation in the simulation depended on a *belief* in key aspects of the social and functional context of their language use – a belief in the *issue*, the *social* (and other) *environment*, the *function* of the role and the *dynamic processes* of the simulation which emerged from the interaction of these.

Simulations have *functional* roles (see the opening pages of Chapter 1). Role function is essential to linguistic behaviour since it provides purpose.

Ami: . . . you feel angry because they want to spoil your village an' that . . . where you live.

Ami was driven by the function of her role in relation to the development issue. Her function was defined by her allotted interest in the community as a resident and as a conservationist. She had a vested interest in relation to the issue.

An essential difference between the simulation and other forms of role play is to do with the *dynamic* which controls and establishes the role function. On many occasions I've 'thrown' a group of school students into a small office as deadlines for GCSE oral assessments approached (in the long and distant past of course!) and said something to the effect of: 'You've just been in a car crash. You were in the car coming this way and you were in the one coming that way. A police officer has now arrived – that's you. Explain who's fault it was to the officer.' A number of things happened in my experience. Those students who didn't say much often *still* didn't but became acutely embarrassed. The discussion wandered aimlessly. There was little clarity about purpose. It didn't really seem to matter – people went through the mechanics of the discussion but never really left the role of 'student crammed in office'. They were very much aware of and performing for the extrinsic purpose – the teacher audience – and the social dynamics of the classroom prevailed.

Definition of and belief in function depends very much not just on the description of a role but how things impinge on that role *over time*. I recall in taking up new posts, how I would at first sit in meetings as an observer on the outside, trying to inject the occasional input according to what I thought was appropriate. I would be emotionally detached where others were vehement, and logically detached where others built arguments on existing social, political and other constructions to which I was not party. I was blind to the basis of much of the interaction. My contributions were as mechanical and *unfelt* as the poor school students in the office. As I came to empty more documents from my pigeon hole each day, undertook tasks, responded and reacted to my environment, my function became defined and meaningful. Much of this definition also depended on locating those with whom I interacted, socially and functionally in terms of the job.

In the same way, the simulation defines role function over time according to how things impinge on the role in a *progressive* or *dynamic* way. Ami was not told 'You are a member of this community and you want to preserve it'. She might have argued a logical case on the basis of a few facts. However, she would *not* have developed the deeply felt set of attitudes and emotions or a sense of purpose – except to do the work with presumably some educational reward or because the teacher asked. Ongoing structures in the simulation and the decisions and behaviour of other participants acted dynamically on Ami to shape her attitudes, feelings and behaviour.

One could see this working on Ami through the simulation. I had started to construct the fiction of the community through some role work. I announced that 'Television South West' would be visiting the village a (simulation) week hence, and that participants should prepare a talk about the village for the cameras. This involved students introducing themselves to each other in role and sharing fictional anecdotes about themselves based on given roles and other documentation. Identities were at this stage being built up, and some very interesting stories were developed. Yet at this stage Ami was little enthused or engaged when, as the vicar, I welcomed the camera crew to the village hall – 'When you was the vicar . . . I just went along with it. I didn't think nothing of it' – and that was despite the improvised work which took place and the development of a plausible environment during the 'filming' of the talks. Things only paid off later: 'When you was the [development representative] I just felt really angry . . .'.

What had happened between the two stages was that Ami had gone from what she saw as 'acting', being a village member doing a talk for the television company, to a fully *functional* role, with a clearly defined, sculpted *purpose*, which was, in her case, to defend her community, which had itself become a 'living' thing in her imagination. And this focused her thoughts: 'normally with acting . . . all you think about is trying to get it all right . . . but in this you really had to think to see what to say and what to do'.

The number of occasions on which Ami and Toni emphasized feelings and attitude as their motivating force should not go unnoticed:

Toni: Yeah and this way [through the simulation] you get to express your *feelings*.
Ami: I just felt really *angry*.

And in explaining Michelle's participation:

Toni: . . . she really got angry . . .
Ami: . . . she was really overreacting.

Toni's first comment here is fundamental. Whereas, as I indicated earlier, Ami was prescribed by emotions derived from her perceived social situation, 'I'm embarrassed . . .', Toni acknowledges how she was liberated by emotions and the means to express these. In the classroom their emotional and thus behavioural status is quite different from when they are together in the playground sharing common and meaningful social experiences and securities. In the simulation they not only escaped the social/emotional confines of the regular classroom experience, 'everyone's looking at me', but they needed to develop feelings and the means to communicate these to use language comfortably.

This important motivation has much to do with the social interaction which is constructed out of Ami's, Toni's and other people's functional roles and the effects their personality and experience in the simulation brings to bear on these. If I can refer to it for one last time in this book, the game of *Monopoly* is a good example of how function affects behaviour. I become extremely volatile when playing *Monopoly* according to how others impinge on my objectives. One can feel great affection for another participant for some disaster which works to one's own advantage and equally feel intense hostility because the chance of dice makes them land on 'Super Tax, £100' instead of Mayfair next door, which one has recently refurbished with a shiny new hotel. I find it hard to understand the utter transformation of my social and (colourful) linguistic behaviour by the end of a game, nor that of my rivals, when I am trying to readjust to the normal social and linguistic reference points we share. Feelings and attitudes become important motivators for this behaviour. In this web of changing and developing emotions and social behaviour every action, every piece of apparatus becomes immensely significant and value-laden.

In the same way the community, and all its aspects which impinged on Ami's function, became something Ami believed in and developed feelings about. Crucially, the dynamics of the community were something she had the *power* to affect – that's what functional roles are all about. The dynamic of the simulation with its interaction of power relationships drew her in more and more.

Deepening functional reality

There is no doubt that the functions of roles in a simulation can lead to powerful engagement through a great emotional intensity and the development of a new social fabric, or at least new rules for social interaction as I have explained. In the simulation I wanted to establish more than functional roles in the sense of 'You are a conservationist'. I wanted to intensify the reality of the simulation. I wanted the social scenario of the community to replace that of the classroom. I wanted participants to invest and identify in a meaningful way with their roles at social and emotional levels as fully as possible. This is why I chose to develop the role and community identities as I have explained with the visit of 'TV South West'.

When the talks were delivered before the 'camera', a whole fabric about individual and community identity was established. Anecdotes linked members of the village, bringing them into individual and group relationships of friendship, conflict and so forth, and extended the individual and community history. The functional roles became more firmly embedded in the social fabric of the community.

Although Ami may not have thought much about the community environment when it was first being established in this way – 'I didn't think nothing of it' – she became emotionally attached to it once her function became apparent, and thus she became angry and wanted to function in some way to preserve it as I've shown. If I'd just said 'Your village is being messed up, do something about it', it is unlikely she would have been so effectively engaged whatever the dynamic. What would she have defended? What *was* this community? When it came to the crunch she was defending 'real' people, 'real' relationships, a 'real' community and she had to have an image of her relationship with these things. In real life, functions, people and scenarios and other elements of the environment carry with them emotional, moral, social and other baggage which manipulates attitudes and action, and simulations can be rather thin in this respect (this point is developed in the last chapter).

In sum, while the functional role may provide the basis for decision-making by participants ('I am a conservationist, therefore . . .'), the emotional experience and the communication this gives rise to may vary according to a complex network of personal, social and other environmental factors constructed in the simulation through role interaction. In this case, extended role-play was incorporated within the simulation.

The improvisation described above might be challenged in that it seems more akin to drama than a simulation. I have no doubt that the reality of simulations can be enhanced by improvisation without being destructive of the simulation itself. For me at least, this activity was well within the bounds of a simulation, since it did not conflict with the predefined functions of the roles in relation to the issue (with one exception below) or with the ongoing structure of the simulation which did not itself develop in an improvised way. There is a need for care that participant improvisation is 'pocketed' so that it will not conflict with the main simulation structures.

There does need to be clear definition of function to achieve any kind of investment from participants in the new social reality. Poor planning on my part made this clear. Ami was given conflicting roles – an industrial occupation on the one hand, but she also developed an interest as a conservationist. This caused her considerable confusion logically and emotionally: 'I felt really funny because . . . the job . . . didn't really help did it because I was killing the birds . . . it just made me feel as if I was saying all the wrong things'. She didn't know how to behave or how to *feel*. She couldn't root herself comfortably in a perspective even though she had the arguments sorted out in her head. As a result she found it difficult to posture, to behave. She then found a solution by defaulting herself to the conservationist perspective, the one which had been built up in the improvised work around the television visit, cancelling out the other conflicting role, and from this point she found it easy to posture. She found an identity in which to embed her arguments. Of course, it may be desirable to include such conflicts in simulations, since they exist for us when our philosophies and actions conflict with each other in real life.

This does, incidentally, also highlight the real danger of mixing drama/role-play with the predefined roles and functions of simulations. This mix, rather than being denied (for reasons I have stated), needs careful handling.

Carter (in Keen 1992: 23) says: 'Language develops most effectively and richly in children out of relationships of trust in open-ended contexts'. Ami was liberated from the old classroom social structures by the invention of new ones. She was able, seemingly, to define *her own* functionality according to the *attitudes* and *feelings* that *she* had. There appeared to her to be no expectation of output, or of a particular response (she was of course manipulated considerably by the structures of the simulation). At the same time, she was not engaged in purely open-ended tasks. The simulation provided, and provides, structure for language experience and variety, and as Toni and Ami showed in the debrief, an opportunity for language awareness and study.

Developing language experience in the simulation

Meaning

Giglioli (1990: 8) explains in his introduction to *Language and Social Context*:

> . . . sociolinguistics has shown that speech is not the haphazard result of mere individual choices, the manifestation of a person's psychological states, but that it is

remarkably patterned ... systematic variations of speech behaviour have been shown to reflect the underlying constraints of a system of social relations.

These patterns determine how one uses language according to the social context in which one finds oneself.

For Halliday (1973: 24), language development was not about just learning the mechanics of language, the rules of the code, but about the social functions for which language is used:

> ... language development needs to be seen as the mastery of linguistic functions. Learning one's mother tongue is learning the uses of language and the meanings, or rather the meaning potential, associated with them. The structures, the words and the sounds are the realisation of this meaning potential. Learning language is learning how to mean.

The meaning potential is the range of possible meanings in any given social situation: 'Speech [takes] place in fairly restricted contexts where the options are limited and the meaning potential is ... rather closely specifiable' (Halliday 1973: 26). Language use is constrained by social rules – or patterns. For Halliday, these change according to the function of the social situation – according to whether one is, to use his example, undertaking a transaction in a shop (p. 26) or, to use my example, acting on jury service. In either case, one can only mean certain things as the main, or essential, part of the function. 'I want a loaf of bread' clearly belongs in one of the contexts, whereas 'Let's look at the evidence' clearly belongs to the other. The social language as well as the meaning is likely to be different in each case and this may extend to dialect, tone and vocabulary, for example. The social and functional meaning, then, uses varieties of language 'appropriate' to the situation.

If we are to prepare children in schools for adult life, it is vital that they experience and study language in the social context, to understand the social powers which act on language and the social powers which are derived from language. It is essential that students learn 'the social consequences of language varieties' (Giglioli 1990: 11) about the power of language in relation to 'appropriate' socio-functional contexts. It is not just that Ami had to unlearn the regular behavioural modes of her classroom, but that she must behave in a range of social situations for language use.

Jones (1982: 8, 10) describes how in adopting the role of judge or diplomat in the simulation, one is learning transferable skills:

> If the participant is a diplomat, then the appropriate language is the language of diplomacy, and the appropriate behaviour includes all those social skills and social remarks which can make the diplomacy more effective ... diplomacy is also useful at home, at work and on holiday.

The simulation thus engages students in those types of social discourse and situation which may serve them in life outside of the classroom. It is not only the job – one is not preparing students to be Judges and Diplomats – but the functional behaviour which matters, so that students can become judges and diplomats.

Functions of language don't occur of course in the simplistic sense that the role of a diplomat in a simulation offers *one* social situation, *one* (set of) meaning potential which might broadly be termed 'diplomacy'. In order to accomplish the overall and changing function of the Diplomat or Judge, the participant has to negotiate a variety of sub-functions, each with their own meaning potentials, their own social consequences. It may be that the diplomat has to negotiate, to censure, to organize, to operate in informal contexts and official ones, individually and in groups, cooperatively and competitively, through the medium of writing and of speech. In each situation, the participant will have to think about the current potential for power (function) in terms of current social and functional relationships. For example, it would be highly inappropriate for a delegate to the UN to engage in idle chit-chat with the international membership about his or her marital problems – this would surely weaken his or her case – yet this might be a very subtle device in winning personal allegiance in the context of small talk in the ante-rooms before a debate. The Diplomat is not just a diplomat, but just as the pupil has the behaviour variety (including language) for the playground and the variety for the classroom, so the role of diplomat has its varieties. Whatever the role of the participant, it is likely that she will experience a range of varieties of functional and social context. It is these meanings and the languaging that grows from this that become transferable. It is the variety of function and situation and the ability to switch and adapt which extends our linguistic abilities: 'Our command of our language extends as we meet new situations and have to find linguistic expression to match the demands they make upon us' (Doughty *et al.* 1971: 10). Indeed, the motivation to achieve the overall goal, or purpose, of the role in relation to the issue, took Ami through a wide range of language experiences in just this way.

During the course of the simulation, she engaged in whole group situations with the television crew and with the development representatives and then small group situations in preparing strategies to deal with the issue. Her talk involved her in cooperative strategy development with her allies, and in confrontational dialogue with her enemies. She undertook collaborative writing in preparing a case against the development. She experienced formal talk and informal talk. She acted with the security of her 'colleagues' and independently. But throughout, she maintained consistency of role. In overhearing her interest group preparing their campaign, hers was not the language of the *student* dealing with these different linguistic contexts ('How long have we got? What do you think we could say?'), but the language (in this case) of the dedicated protester: 'I think most people will agree that they moved in [to the village] for quiet . . . A lot of people will just move out'. And this text was accompanied by the body language which had an 'appropriateness' for the differing social and meaning contexts, in this case the shrugging of shoulders, the twisting of the lip in disapproval during the small group analysis of the issue; in others, like the large meetings, through the outward gesturing of hand movements and projecting chin. Such experiences can be constructed in the simulation (by the organization, for example, of big meetings), though often it will be the participants themselves who decided the appropriate course or language varieties within a given 'functional space'.

In the context of discussion of simulations, Taylor and Walford (1978: 25) identified as early as the 1970s a 'so-called "conservative backlash" . . . drawing attention to the need to maintain certain basic skills when, *at the same time*, schools are now pursuing more ambitious intellectual and social objectives for the children in their care'. The climate has hardly abated in the 1980s and 1990s, and Taylor and Walford's (1978: 25) reassurance that 'pupils make greater efforts to read, speak and calculate than they have ever done before because of their motivation within the exercise to hand', is easily confirmed by Ami's experiences in the simulation.

And further, the simulation, in subordinating varieties of communication to a common purpose, achieves a harmony of oracy – speech, reading, writing and listening are closely interactive and interconnected, one giving meaning to the other. The dismemberment of elements of communication, such as the subordination of speech to the pre-eminent literacy, which has in the past provided such a destructive route to learning, and which has threatened to rear its ugly head in recent times, has no place in the simulation.

In terms of functions of language, the matter is more complex than I have described above. In the simulation in which Ami and Toni took part, it was not just a matter of matching up language with meaning according to a range of functional varieties of situation – as in the shop transaction or UN meeting. The simulation showed clearly that the meaning potential in apparently similar functional contexts could be quite different. Given two visits from development representatives to the village, each with similar objectives, the behaviour of the villagers was *quite* different in each case. The first representative was arrogant, not a great listener, uninformed and gave a bit of a sales pitch. The response of the villagers was defiance, to use group solidarity by confirming each others' opinions and developing a group language in which members adopted similar hostile tones and gestures. Tuts and sarcasm became the order of the day and condescension became the name of the game for some: 'Now listen young man!', 'This is supposed to be a *quiet* village! We don't need all these new buildings'. Their attitude had developed out of frustration and perceptions of unsatisfactory behaviour on the part of the visitor. They were learning to fence.

This was the language of power and the power of language (or of the meaning potential) for that *particular* context. Even though there were functional limitations on the possible meanings, as described by Halliday, because of the nature of the business at hand, the language available to achieve objectives was to a significant degree unpredictable. This is shown by the quite different behaviour which took place during a visit from a second representative. Here the representative was willing to listen, courteous, considerate and informed. His speech was modulated and his strategies conciliatory. Within moments he declared a concern about public opinion and that the company would not risk riding roughshod over the population, quite honestly declaring that the company would not wish to become unpopular, especially given the presence of the television cameras. He summed up his approach thus: 'We obviously want to carry you with us'.

Although the group identified him as a different person (I took both roles but they referred to 'the other bloke'), the social behaviour began on their part as it had left off with the first representative. In a short time though the group calmed and adopted the language and behaviour of conciliation, offering points for consideration in a reciprocal relationship. The students used each situation to their best advantage by modifying their behaviour in trying to establish the best means of achieving power according to the unpredictable social dynamic of the situation. Their behaviour (or forms of power) developed and modified as the meaning potential grew according to the social dynamics of each situation (as these forms of power became allowed). They discovered the powers of language by exploration of what was effective in the particular circumstance. The language of condescension would have been powerless and dysfunctional in the second situation.

As Keen (1992: 2) notes, 'The quality of speaking also depends on the nature of the *whole interaction* [my emphasis] to which it contributes', and this includes the peculiarities of interpersonal behaviour for any given functional situation. It is important to learn transferable skills in this sense as well as in the more formal sense of what one might call 'functional varieties' (the shop transaction or the UN meeting or even the informal discussion in the ante-room). The subtext of social relations and attitude in the simulation was as important a function for language as the development issue. This also contributed to defining effective and permissible meaning potential.

Whereas children, according to Halliday (1973: 34), get their image of language from simple functions, for adults, 'Every ... linguistic act, with a few broadly specifiable exceptions, is serving more than one function at once'. He gives the example of a football fan using the word 'trounced' to another fan which has several meanings, including *beat*, *pleasure* at this, and others based on their shared experience (pp. 34–5) – this could even be extended to shared humour at what the club has done in the past (being 'trounced' may be a regular event for them). These meanings depend on the norms of the speech community, of the speaker and hearer and their shared experience of this community, and of each other and the situation in which the event takes place.

Because of the complexity of meanings according to these factors, children are in the game of learning 'linguistic reflexes' (Halliday 1973: 36). It is inconceivable that the simultaneous multiple meanings ('multivalence': ibid.: p. 35) of 'trounced' could have been considered and worked through at the time of speech. Language development thus has to be learned as other *behaviours* through *experience* (in social/functional context) as Flowers (in Shepherd 1993: 1) suggests: 'We learn to skate on the ice and to swim in the water, not in the classroom. Similarly we learn to speak and write our mother tongue in the full context of our daily usage'. In this case, in the context of the shared experience of the simulation.

Jones has described the simulation as 'cohesive'. This means the simulation brings participants together in interaction to resolve the issue or problem at hand (Jones 1982: 7). In terms of language this provides audience and constant feedback. In the collision and cooperation of functions (or of needs), participants can probe and modify their behaviour in the way I've described. In the simulation it was clear, for example, that when condescension ('Now listen young man!') would not be effective, this as a means of (achieving) power was discontinued. The effectiveness of group solidarity seemed to carry lots of power and thus grew, as did the increasing use of a formal accent and register. Behaviour in the simulation was constantly being *tested* by the social context, by the behaviour of other participants. This *sense* of audience, as well as the actual response of the audience, is critical to a sense of purpose and to the nature of discourse.

I mentioned in earlier chapters that the controller can exist in the simulation as a document in role. In this simulation, I was allowed considerable management of the language experience because of the roles I had. As two representatives as I have explained, I achieved quite different sorts of language environment for the participants to respond to. I was able to manipulate first from a position of arrogance, inconsistency and lack of respect. This was designed to 'wind the participants up'. I got in return indignation, and group solidarity through the vested interest I had created in them of defence. My second role exuded confidence, it was authoritative, informed and calm. As I explained earlier, the response to this shifted significantly to reciprocation and conciliation. The kind of permission given by the controller in role, of which I spoke with warning in Chapter 4, can thus be used to advantage.

The debrief might explore

- What was the difference between the representatives?
- How did you react to the first? Why? How did you react to the second? Why?
- Did you respond to what they had to say or how they said it?
- How else could you have responded to this man at this point?
- Would one always respond in this way?

Language and 'reality'

A lot of important work has been done in English teaching to bring the language use of the wider society into the classroom. In the introduction to *Language in Use*, an important step in this direction in the 1970s, Doughty *et al.*, as previously cited, (1971: 10) state that 'Our command of our language extends as we meet new situations and have to find linguistic expression to match the demands they make upon us', and that 'It is therefore necessary that the conditions for using language in school *be similar to those in the world outside* if they are to have any effect on children's competence' (my emphasis). The *Language in Use* project included themes such as 'Language and Culture' and 'Language in Social Organizations', with everyday material being brought into the classroom. A unit on 'Technical Terms' (p. 181) suggests that the teacher (p. 182) 'Ask the class to bring in a collection of recipes from as many sources as possible'.

Clearly one is able to extend the social and functional environment of the classroom as I have shown. Is one, though, recreating the socio-functional contexts of wider society in a simulation? If one says 'You're a judge', upon what will the social and functional criteria be based, in the participant's mind, for her behaviour? It may be that she has seen *Crown Court* on a faded video-recording, or *LA Law* to give a more modern equivalent. But even then the behaviours in these two legal systems are quite different from each other in terms of ritual, including respect for the judge, linguistic interaction and so forth.

Doughty *et al.* (1971: 11) argue that:

> Pupils bring to the class-room a native speaker's knowledge of, and intuitions about, language and its place in human society. In this sense, it is the task of the English teacher not to impart a body of knowledge, but to work upon, develop, refine, and clarify the knowledge and intuitions that his pupils already possess.

Indeed, this was the very source of the work in the simulation described in this chapter. The language experience was based on student assumptions about how a community and its members *might* behave in a certain situation. It became clear, for example, that power through language could be achieved if certain strategies were adopted, as I have described. However, it also risks providing interaction which may be inappropriate in wider society, or in preparing for that wider society. Simulations, in my experience, invariably draw out stereotypical images of roles and situations. In the simulation in which Ami took part, one role was that of vicar (in addition to my own). The role was seriously affected, not very different from a television interpretation of the clerical stereotype played by Derek Nimmo which some readers may remember, although this was probably before the students' time. The role was meek, the language eccentrically 'posh' and drawn out, and quite unlike any real vicar I have heard or met in the real world. Anything slightly rural is likely to be littered with 'Ooh Aaars' and facial contortions close to constipative strain.

In addition, some strategies which achieve power in the simulation might be considered unsavoury or unsatisfactory if applied in the real world. For example, would threats of violence, if they occurred with effect, be acceptable? Would the rules learned in the classroom, effective there, be appropriate or effective in the wider culture? How much should one rely on pupils' (adults'?) often stereotypical, simplistic, compartmentalized views of language and other behaviours?

A language simulation has to explore a variety of functional and social norms for language use in society. Eagleton (1983: 6–7) shows how a passenger can only understand an underground sign 'Dogs must be carried on the escalator' (you cannot go on the escalator without a dog?) because of awareness of the social and functional norms in that context or, as he puts it, 'conventions of reading'. This knowledge comes not from the specific social/functional context of the underground system, or some innate Chomsky-like ability to know the code, but from familiarity with other formal notices in our experience such as those in parks which say 'Keep off the grass'. For the same reason, the social context of my small terraced garden and its social meaning may lead to mockery if such a sign were placed there.

It is not enough to work only from the language experience which children bring to the classroom, although this should be the starting point.

Although students do bring to the classroom intuitions and knowledge about language in the social contexts of the wider world, this can be extended in the way *Language in Use* works. Social and functional models can be imported into the classroom through the simulation. Such devices could be included in the simulation as models for behaviour; for example, by showing a video of *LA Law* prior to the simulation or in other documentation used in the simulation. In historical simulations, I have included contemporaneous documentation, along the lines of the Royal Commission report in Chapter 2, opening up conventions about the socio-linguistic behaviour of the time, place and social group, which has then generated output – letters of protest and speeches, for example – with 'functional appropriateness'.

The debrief also provides an opportunity for analysis of what might seem appropriate and what might not. The student expectations for the behaviour of a judge, however misinformed, is not irrelevant, and like the possible irrelevance of *LA Law* to the British legal system, which I'm sure crossed the mind of some readers, can provide important comparative material for discussion in the debrief. Who is to say that the norms of the wider society should be acceptable? Can't a participant recognize the inadequacy of socio-functional behaviour in a British court as opposed to an American one? What is important is that we start from the student perspective of language behaviour in the simulation. Any prejudices or misconceptions can be explored further in analysis of the behaviour in the simulation during the debrief.

Ami and Toni's own analyses give substance to Keen (1992), from whom I can't resist one last quote: 'language study is a human discipline rooted in language experience' (p. 3).

7 Issues of control and reality

Two significant and celebrated themes in the simulation world, and in this book, are those of *control* and *reality*. This final chapter offers some words of caution about the limitations of these two fundamental aspects of the simulation.

Control

In Chapter 1, I described briefly how students in simulations are empowered through a reduction of the teacher role. I made the point there – and this has been implicit throughout the book – that participants function autonomously within the given simulation structure and that this provides intrinsic, experiential learning and greatly enhances motivation. Because of this 'autonomy' simulations have been heralded as mechanisms which reduce the control and authority of the teacher and enhance those of the learners or participants. This view has much to do with a specious perception that the absence of the teacher from the action (and interaction) of the simulation diminishes his or her power.

A much more dangerous form of control in fact exists in this form of learning than one might find in a classroom with a well-worn dais. For while the participants are absorbed in the reality of the simulation, they are blinded to the *external* reality of control and manipulation by the simulation author and controller, although the latter may herself be the object of such manipulation.

The structure of the simulation has enormous power over those who function within it. The structure may give weight to certain roles according to their function in a simulation or give weight to certain perspectives on an issue by, for example, the way information is distributed to participants, the number of people representing a perspective, who the people are, or in what circumstances they are allowed to communicate. A community leader might have more power because of her social standing in the simulation, or opportunities for expression than other members of the community. Supposing the former represented one political party and the latter another? Simulations manipulate feelings and thoughts and can be used to deliver messages (about racism or the unfairness of trading relations) and it may be that these messages are not always the conscious objective of a designer. I have no doubts about the values which I wanted to convey in the *Roll of Thunder* simulation relating to issues of justice. No honest simulation author could deny conscious or unconscious transmission of values. In any case, the author decides the agenda to a great extent – the information to be seen, who should see it, what kind of interaction occurs and so forth.

Participants often see the rules and mechanisms of the simulation as absolute and not to be questioned. Depending on the kind of simulation and the context in which it is used, it can be difficult for them to examine the power of the roles they have been given or to show awareness of more subliminal elements of control which they have no power or authority to define. Indeed, such deconstruction after the event has come as complete revelation when raised in debriefs. Sharrock and Watson (1987: 37–8) have identified this as 'submerged power authority', which they liken at times (when a participant is used as controller in the simulation in the role, for example, of chairperson) to colonial 'indirect rule' operated through indigenous puppets. The often *unseen* authority of the simulation is, I believe, even more submerged than this.

In Chapter 1, I suggested that systems simulations exercise more control over participants than communications simulations. I described participants with regard to systems simulations as being 'pushed from pillar to post' – the variables for action and outcomes being largely predefined by the author. However, I would suggest that the communications simulation is of a potentially more *dangerous* kind because of its greater *sense* of participant control. The assumption is more easily made that the simulation is being defined by the participants because of the comparatively loose structure such as I described it in Chapter 1. Simulations based on authors' detailed models of reality, such as *Blood Money*, exercise control in a more overt way. Of *Blood Money*, Greenblat (1987: 25) says: 'We identified the most important factors to be simulated, and generated a second list of factors we wanted to be emergent in most runs of the game'.

The debrief is more likely here, I would suggest, to lead to questions about the author's interpretation and its more obvious rules and mechanisms. It is more definably something imposed. The simulation described in Chapter 3, based on Mildred D. Taylor's (1990) *Roll of Thunder, Hear My Cry*, belongs to this latter genre of simulation and was designed so that participants could challenge its construction in the debrief. It was based on a model of my perception of the author's reality to be compared and contrasted with the participants' perception of that reality. Participants were able to be critical of the simulation structure in terms of their understanding of the book.

I would not wish to appear entirely cynical about control and manipulation through simulations. One simply has to recognize that it is there and that it needs to be used carefully. The fact that this control exists does not undermine the experiential and intrinsic nature and value of the simulation as I discussed them in Chapter 1 – but these should not be mistaken as necessarily a concomitant freedom from authority. The simulation can be a dangerous medium and issues need to be considered carefully.

Reality

One argument for using simulations in schools, as I suggested in Chapter 1, is that the work of the classroom can be tied more closely to the reality of the outside world. Andersen (1987) has described a 'reality gap' in relation to simulations based on so-called 'models of reality'. Greenblat (1987: 25), in describing how she and John Gagnon developed *Blood Money*, explains how they took (and designers in general take) a *'substantive content* of the real world system' – a discrete, unitary set of relationships which will function independently as a system in the simulation.

The extraction of a segment from reality provides all sorts of problems in terms of representing that reality. *Nothing is substantive*. As Andersen (1987) points out, a role in real life does not begin with the job simulated, but is predefined by the motives for taking the job and wider relationships with the real world which cannot be incorporated into the simulation:

> ... decision-making takes place *in media res* in the midst of the hurly burly of daily business life and is therefore connected to and located among all the other business activities which executives engage in; holding and attending meetings, dealing with paperwork, making phone calls and the like ... Business activities are continuous with other social activities and are entwined with them.
>
> (Andersen 1987: 47)

This is a problem I wrestled with in developing the *Roll of Thunder* simulation in Chapter 3. As I described in that chapter, I tried to separate an economic system from a wider social (racist) system, which in the text had a significant impact on how the economic system worked. In many respects, this was a most unsatisfactory compromise, as I have explained.

In simulations which purport to be based on models of reality, there is a further 'reality gap' (discussed in Sharrock and Watson 1987: 39), for the simulation is not at all a reality but an author's perception of reality. This is going to be particularly the case with systems simulations where the designer has much more control over the environment (see Chapter 1).

This has implications, too, for communications simulations. If the objective is to allow children in the classroom to explore wider social contexts for language use, wider social *realities* are not going to be achieved. Here is merely a shift in ownership. Instead of the simulation author bringing her perception of reality to the classroom, the participants will bring theirs based on whatever experience they have of the outside world. Often their representation of that experience is shrouded in stereotype both of role and situation. In a simulation I ran not unlike that which opened Chapter 1, one pair of participants were given the role set of shopowners. It didn't take long for these participants to define their role and language in terms of a caricature of 'Pakistani corner shop owners'. Communications simulations which attempt to represent the real world are often littered with such participant distortions.

This is not an argument against the use of simulations and not an argument against the use of simulations to bring the processes of the classroom closer to those of the real world. It is, however, important to be aware of these limitations. Simulations still provide opportunities to develop transferable skills through the challenges of a variety of linguistic and other problem-solving situations, as I described in Chapter 6. The real world can be examined in a comparative sense – 'Is that how it would have happened?', 'Was that the right kind of language for that situation?' – through the all-important debrief. Simulations (should) provide enough of a comparative structure for this to be possible. The simulation is a means to examine the real world and is not the reality itself. And while an awareness of the 'real' world is important, the development of transferable skills is more critical. It is important not so much to prepare or train children for the real world, as to prepare them to be flexible in a world where there is different appropriateness for the same kinds of function in different places – and in a world of changing communicative and social expectations and problem-solving contexts.

References

Books

Andersen, R.J. (1987) The reality problem in games and simulations. In Crookall, D. *et al.* (eds), *Simulation – Gaming in the Late 1980s*. Proceedings of the International Simulation and Gaming Association's 17th International Conference. Oxford, Pergamon Press.

Davis, K. and Hollowell, J. (eds) (1977) *Inventing and Playing Games in the English Classroom: A Handbook for Teachers*. Urbana, IL, National Council for Teachers of English.

Doughty, P., Pearce, J. and Thornton, G. (1971) *Language in Use*. London, Edward Arnold.

Eagleton, T. (1983) *Literary Theory: An Introduction*. Oxford, Blackwell.

Giglioli, P.P. (ed.) (1990) *Language and Social Context*. Harmondsworth, Penguin.

Greenblat, C.S. (1987) Communicating about simulation design. In Crookall, D. *et al.* (eds), *Simulation – Gaming in the Late 1980s*. Proceedings of the International Simulation and Gaming Association's 17th International Conference. Oxford, Pergamon Press.

Halliday, M.A.K. (1973) *Explorations in the Functions of Language*. London, Edward Arnold.

Handcock, W.D. (ed.) (1977) *English Historical Documents*, Vol. XII(2) 1874–1914. London, Eyre and Spottiswoode.

Jones, K. (1982) *Simulations in Language Teaching*. Cambridge, Cambridge University Press.

Jones, K. (1985) *Designing Your Own Simulations*. London, Methuen.

Jones, K. (1987) *Simulations: A Handbook for Teachers and Trainers*, 2nd edn. London, Kogan Page.

Keen, J. (1992) *Language and the English Curriculum*. Milton Keynes, Open University Press.

Lingard, J. (1972) *Across the Barricades*. London, Penguin.

Sharrock, W.W. and Watson, D.R. (1987) 'Power' and 'realism' in simulation and gaming: Some pedagogic and analytic observations. In Crookall, D. *et al.* (eds), *Simulation – Gaming in the Late 1980s*. Proceedings of the International Simulation and Gaming Association's 17th International Conference. Oxford, Pergamon Press.

Shepherd, V. (1993) *Playing the Language Game*. Milton Keynes, Open Univerity Press.
Tansey, P.J. and Unwin, D. (1969) *Simulation and Gaming in Education*. London, Methuen.
Taylor, J. and Walford, R. (1978) *Learning and the Simulation Game*. Milton Keynes, Open University Press.
Taylor, M.D. (1990) *Roll of Thunder, Hear My Cry*. Oxford, Heinemann New Windmills.
Thatcher, D. and Robinson, J. (1986) *An Introduction to Simulations and Games in Education*. Fareham, Solent Simulations.

Simulations/Games

Cluedo (1990) Leeds, Waddington Games.
Greenblat, C.S. (1975) *Blood Money*. Bethesda, MD, OPCE.
Monopoly (1936) London, John Waddington Ltd.
Shirts, G. (1969) *Starpower*. Del Mar, CA, Simile II.
Shirts, G. (1976) *Bafa Bafa*. Del Mar, CA, Simile II.
Trading Game (n.d.) London, Christian Aid.

Index

accounting, 37, 47
Across the Barricades (J. Lingard), 28
action, during the, 72–4
Andersen, R. J., 100
attitude
    attitude shaping behaviour, 88, 90, 94
    shaping attitude, 35, 46, 49, 65–6, 69, 87, 89, 93
audience, 22, 26, 87, 95
autonomy, 14–15, 98

Bafa Bafa (G. Shirts), 20
basic skills, 93
Blood Money (C. S. Greenblat), 16–17, 18–19, 37, 99, 100
briefing
    general, 30–2, 70–2, 73
    Roll of Thunder, 49, 63

Capjefos (C. S. Greenblat), 24
caricature, 35, 44, 73, 101
    see also stereotyping
Carter, D., 90
Chomsky, N., 97
Cluedo (Waddington Games), 31
Coleman, B., 17
controller
    function, 14, 36, 71, 72–4, 77
    intrinsic controlling, 32–3, 49, 73
    see also documents

Davis, K., 18
dialect, 25, 85, 91

documents
    access to, 33–4, 37, 38, 49, 69, 72
    controller's, 32–4, 48–50, 61–4
    controller as document, 27, 28, 31, 32–3, 35, 95
    developing, 28–36
    intrinsic/extrinsic, 28–33, 49–50, 70–1
    Roll of Thunder, 29–30, 47–64
Doughty, P., 92, 95–6
    see also Language in Use

Eagleton, T., 96–7
emotions, *see* feelings
empathy, 14, 17, 21, 31, 34–5, 45, 46–7, 80, 82

feelings
    arousing, 44, 46–7, 68, 82, 84–90
    debriefing, 75–6, 77, 78, 79
Flower, F. D., 94
Front Page (K. Jones), 20–1, 37

Giglioli, P. P., 90–1
Greenblat, C. S., 43, 99
    see also Blood Money
Guezkow, H., 18

Halliday, M. A. K., 91, 93, 94
Hollowell, J., 18

Jones, K., 16, 18, 21, 22–4, 31–2, 77, 91, 95

Keen, J., 19, 85, 94, 97

language varieties, 86, 91–4,
language and reality, 95–7
Language in Use, 92, 95–7

Monopoly (J. Waddington Ltd), 16–17, 31, 34, 37, 64, 88
motivation, 15–16, 46–7, 73, 84–90, 98

oracy, 93

Quantum Leap, 31

Robinson, J., 17, 18
roles
   allocation, 28–31, 38, 50, 62, 70–2
   continuity, 38, 70, 92
   planning, 34–7
   reroling/deroling, 76–8, 82
role play, 15, 16, 35, 86–7, 88, 89–90
Royal Commission on Poorer Classes in Ireland, 25–7, 97

secrecy, 69, 71, 73
setting up, 62, 68–70
Sharrock, W. W., 18, 99, 100
simulations
   communications
      control, 99
   definitions, 15–17, 18–19
   designing, 21–7
   designing *Roll of Thunder*, 41–4, 68
   reality, 100
gaming, 44
systems
   control, 99
   definitions, 15–17, 18–19
   designing, 21–4, 27–8, 34, 35, 36, 38
   designing *Roll of Thunder*, 41–4, 64, 66
   reality, 100
stereotyping, 96, 100–1
   see also caricature

Tansey, P. J., 73
Taylor, J., 18, 23
   see also basic skills
timing, 64–5
Thatcher, D., 17, 18
Trading Game, 20, 36
transferable skills, 19, 91–2, 94

Unwin, D., 73

Walford, R., 18, 23
Watson, D. R., 18, 99, 100

DESCRIBING LANGUAGE (Second Edition)
David Graddol, Jenny Cheshire and Joan Swann

A student introduction to descriptive linguistics, *Describing Language* is essentially practical in its orientation. It is useful for anyone who wishes to refer to technical literature involving linguistic description, who requires a basic conceptual framework and technical vocabulary with which to discuss language, and who needs to make elementary but principled descriptions and analyses of real data (such as classroom interaction or counselling sessions). Topics covered include phonetics, prosody, word structure, syntax, text and discourse structure, word and utterance meaning, and non-verbal behaviour.

This is a significantly revised, updated and expanded version of the successful first edition. In particular, it uses a new approach to syntax and a broader review of grammar including an accessible introduction to both Chomsky's Universal Grammar and Halliday's Systemic Grammar. It is an invaluable textbook for students across the social sciences

Contents
Introduction – The nature of language – The sounds of language – Sentence and word structure – Meaning – Writing systems – Face to face interaction – Discourse and text – Appendix – References – Index.

256pp   0 335 19315 3 (Paperback)

ENGLISH PEOPLE
THE EXPERIENCE OF TEACHING AND LEARNING ENGLISH IN BRITISH UNIVERSITIES

Colin Evans

English People is a portrait of the subject 'English' as it is experienced by teachers and students in British Higher Education. The author has interviewed staff and students in the Universities of Cardiff, Newcastle, Oxford and Stirling and in the former Polytechnic of North London (now the University of North London). These 'English People' speak of the impact of Theory, of Feminism, of the experience of reading and writing, of the problems of teaching literature, of the peculiarities of Oxford and of compulsory Anglo-Saxon, of post-colonial literature and of academic leadership in a time of financial pressure.

English People is also an example of the way in which nations attempt to produce unity out of ethnic diversity by using the national education system and especially the subject which has the name of the national language. It questions whether 'English' can still produce unity and whether it has unity itself. Is 'English', like the British Isles, a varied archipelago and not a land mass? Has it deconstructed itself out of existence?

The book is about students and teachers who have made this choice of subject and career, and is fascinating reading for past, present and aspiring students and teachers of English, in universities, colleges and schools. It is also relevant to anyone interested in Higher Education and its organization.

Contents
Part 1: Joining – Origins – Choice – Reading and writing – Teaching and learning – Life in an institution – Part 2: Dividing – Male/female – Theory – Discipline – English, Englishes and the English – Postface – Appendix – Notes – Bibliography – Index.

256pp   0 335 09359 0 (Paperback)   0 335 09361 2 (Hardback)

A SCHOOLING IN 'ENGLISH'
CRITICAL EPISODES IN THE STRUGGLE TO SHAPE LITERARY AND CULTURAL STUDIES

John Dixon

This places the formation and reformations of 'English' in higher education through three periods and movements crucial to the development of the discipline: the University Extension movement in the late nineteenth century; Cambridge English in the 1920s; and the widening of literary and cultural studies in the 1960s and early 1970s. In each of these periods English studies were swept forward by creative energies from below (from students and their aspirations) as well as by networks of radical academics and enabling institutional structures. John Dixon explores the historical and cultural contexts, the institutional barriers and opportunities, the key figures and their discourses, and the coexistence of contrary traditions and movements. He traces how and why Modern Literature was taught in its formative years, the emergence of Richards and Empson, and the flowering of cultural studies; he analyses the significance of each turning point for the past and present of literary and cultural studies.

Contents
Placing academic subjects, culturally and historically – Part 1: The University Extension 1867–92 – The democratic movement for a peripatetic university – Programmes and practices for a new subject – Efforts to theorize teaching and learning – Inventing discourses for a new project – Change at the centre of academic power – Literature and society: a different view – Part 2: Cambridge 1919–29 – A space, and demand, for reconstruction – New directions of theoretical interest – Experimental investigations in an English course – New discursive options and theories – A brake on innovation, despite new demands – A revolutionary theoretical alternative – Part 3: Restructuring an elite system 1960–79 – Pressures for radical change in education – Theoretical guidance for new approaches – A second phase: rebellions, challenges and liberation – Into dialogue, but against the grain – Reading as dialogue, but against the grain – Reading as dialogue in a social context – Lessons for the future? – Bibliography and references – Name index – Subject index.

240pp   0 335 09321 3 (Paperback)   0 335 09322 1 (Hardback)